The Fine Arts Cookbook II

 Distributed by CBI Publishing Company, Inc.

MUSEUM OF FINE ARTS · BOSTON, MASSACHUSETTS

Cover and title page illustration:
GUSTAVE CAILLEBOTTE (French, 1848-1894)
Fruit Displayed on a Stand. Oil painting
Fanny P. Mason Fund

Contents

Preface

Volume II of the *Fine Arts Cookbook* is
an extension of the fine art of dining so
well put forth in Volume I, published in
1970, but with greater emphasis on dishes
that can be prepared ahead, the best of
recipes brought back from foreign travels,
treasured recipes passed down through
Museum families, and a guide to wines by
the connoisseur-husband of a Ladies'
Committee member.

From the many hundreds of recipes sub-
mitted, we have selected 300 of the very
best. They come from past and present
members of the Ladies' Committee, from
curators, staff, gallery instructors, trustees,
and the Museum Restaurant. Having tested
and tasted every single dish, we assure
you they will truly bring pleasure to your
own dining.

Foreword

For Museum visitors who have culinary as well as artistic interests, I am pleased to introduce the second volume of the *Fine Arts Cookbook*. Since it was first published ten years ago, several printings of thousands of copies have found their way into the kitchens of our Members and friends. The enormous popularity of this collection of recipes calls for a new selection and demonstrates again the boundless versatility of the "Museum family."

The actor Sacha Guitry once sent a postcard to Fernand Point, chef at the famous French Restaurant de la Pyramide, saying: "Wherever I am in the world, whenever I have a bad meal, I think of you, just as wherever I have a good meal, I think of you as well." If the second volume of the *Fine Arts Cookbook* could inspire a similar tribute, those who worked so diligently to make it a success would feel that they have achieved their objective.

JAN FONTEIN
Director

Prologues

Maine Shrimp Spread

"Adapted from several summer-in-Maine recipes. I usually double the recipe. Very popular at parties."

Yield: 1¼ cups

1 (3-ounce) package cream cheese
¼ cup mayonnaise
1 teaspoon red onion, minced
1 tablespoon catsup
Tabasco (optional)
paprika
1 (4½-ounce) can small shrimp, drained

Thoroughly mix all the ingredients except shrimp./Fold in the shrimp./Chill several hours before serving.

Mrs. Harold H. Lounsberry,
Ladies' Committee Associate

Cheese Puffs

"These disappear fast."

Yield: 24 or more

1 cup mayonnaise
⅓ cup Parmesan cheese, grated
1 small onion, chopped very fine
24 rounds white bread

Mix first three ingredients together./Cut thin-sliced white bread in small rounds and toast on one side./Spread untoasted side with mayonnaise mixture and put under broiler until golden.

Variation: Our hostess in Santa Barbara put a slice of cherry tomato on the toast rounds before adding the mayonnaise and sprinkled the top with Parmesan./Also, oregano was added to the mayonnaise.

Mrs. George N. Proctor,
Ladies' Committee Associate

Cheese Onion Hors d'Oeuvre

"Make plenty!"

Yield: 48 squares

1 cup onion, chopped
¼ cup butter
1½ cups prepared biscuit mix
1 cup milk
1 egg, beaten
10 ounces cheddar cheese, grated
2 tablespoons sesame seeds (optional)

Sauté onion in butter until transparent; add to biscuit mix along with milk, egg, and half the cheese./In a buttered 9 x 13-inch pan, spread half the batter, sprinkle over it half the remaining cheese, cover with rest of batter./Sprinkle with remaining cheese (and sesame seeds, if desired)./Bake 25 minutes in 350° oven./Cool before cutting. (Freezes well.)

Mrs. John B. Sears,
Ladies' Committee

Herring Italian Style

"Mediterranean flavor."

Serves 6-8

2 (12-ounce) jars herring in wine sauce
½ red onion
2 large ripe tomatoes or 1 can Italian plum tomatoes, drained
½ cup black olives, pitted and sliced
1 jar chili sauce

Drain herring, reserve juice, and cut, if necessary, into bite-size pieces./Cut onions and tomatoes into cubes./Add to herring along with olives and ½-¾ jar of chili sauce./ Add herring juice if more liquid is needed. Marinate overnight./Serve with dark rye bread or on lettuce-lined platter.

Barbara Stern Shapiro,
Assistant Curator, Prints,
Drawings, and Photographs

Roquefort-Bacon Pinwheels

"Prepare ahead and broil as needed."

Yield: 30

1 loaf bread, thin-sliced
¼ pound Roquefort cheese
¼ pound butter or margarine
¼ pound bacon, cut in strips, 3 strips
**   to the slice**

Cut crusts from bread./Mix Roquefort and butter./Spread on bread slices and roll, holding together with bacon wrapped around and nailed with a toothpick./Broil, turning to cook on all sides.

Mrs. Frederick Costanza,
Ladies' Committee Associate

Sweet Pepper and Blue Cheese Canapé

"Tempting to look at, more tempting to eat."

Yield: 16 rounds

3 not-too-large sweet peppers, preferably
**   red, or 6-8 long, green Italian peppers**
6 ounces cream cheese, softened
¼ cup packed blue cheese
1 tablespoon onion, grated
2 tablespoons butter
salt
toast rounds, buttered

Slice off core ends of peppers./Cut off another thin slice from bottom of each pepper./Remove seeds./Blend cream cheese, blue cheese, grated onion, butter, and salt thoroughly in blender./Stuff peppers with mixture, filling them well, using a spatula./Refrigerate until the filling becomes firm./Neatly slice into ¼-inch slices and serve on buttered toast rounds.

Suzanne Chapman,
Associate Curator Emeritus,
Egyptian and Ancient Near Eastern Art

Baba Ghanoush

"Smashing success with cocktails!"

Serves 6-8

1 large eggplant
2 cloves garlic
2 tablespoons lemon juice
¼ cup tahini (ground sesame-seed paste)
¼ tablespoon ground cumin (or more)
salt
1 tablespoon parsley, chopped
olive oil
onion, grated
lemon wedges

Place eggplant under broiler or over charcoal fire and cook until soft and skin is blistered and blackened, turning frequently (about 10-20 minutes)./As soon as it is cool enough to handle, peel off skin and drain off excess juices, squeezing gently./Blend in food processor with garlic cloves until fairly smooth, then add lemon juice, tahini, cumin, salt, and parsley and mix well./Serve as a dip with torn pita (Syrian) bread./Surround with lemon wedges, and dribble a little olive oil and grated onion over top of dip before serving.

Larry Salmon,
Former Curator, Textiles

- **Drain a can of plain artichokes and marinate overnight in good Italian dressing.**

- **Stuff celery with 2 parts cream cheese, 1 part blue cheese, a crushed garlic clove, and a dash of Worcestershire.**

- **Norwegian *Pultoast* is a delicious spread. Finely shred coon cheese, cover it with beer, and let it stand several hours. Work in a generous sprinkle of caraway seeds, blend until smooth, and refrigerate.**

Crunchy Parmesan Sticks

"Make-ahead hors d'oeuvre. The only way to keep these is to hide them!"

Yield: 32 sticks

8 slices bread, thin-sliced
1 stick butter, melted
½ cup Cornflakes, crushed (or Special K or Total)
½ cup Parmesan cheese, freshly grated
¼ rounded teaspoon garlic salt

Remove crusts./Cut bread slices into 4 sticks./Dunk into butter./Roll in mixture of cereal crumbs, cheese, and garlic salt./Place on ungreased cookie sheet./Bake 10 to 15 minutes at 325°./Put on waxed paper to cool./Store in tightly covered tin.

Mrs. Henry Brown,
Ladies' Committee Associate

Hot Artichoke Hors d'Oeuvre

"This year's rage at our cocktail parties."

Serves 6-8

1 (1-pound) can artichoke hearts, cut into pieces
1 cup Hellmann's mayonnaise (other brands may separate in baking)
¼ – ½ cup Parmesan cheese, grated

Mix ingredients together./Put in an ovenproof casserole dish and bake at 350° about 20 minutes or until bubbly./Add a dash of paprika on top for color./Serve with crackers.

Mrs. Malcolm L. Trayser,
Ladies' Committee Associate

• **Wrap thin slices of prosciutto around brazil nuts for a quick munch.**

Nachos Speciales

"They disappear as fast as they are made!"

1 package large-size Fritos
American or cheddar cheese slices
Jalapeño peppers (canned)

Put about a quarter slice cheese on each Frito, and top with a small piece of Jalapeño./Place on cookie sheet./Bake at about 400° until cheese melts, about 5 minutes.

Mrs. Frederick Costanza,
Ladies' Committee Associate

Hummus with Sesame Seeds

"We had this on a Turkish boat sailing around Greek islands."

Serves 6

¾ cup sesame seeds, toasted deep golden brown
2 tablespoons olive or vegetable oil
1 (16-ounce) can garbanzos
2 cloves garlic, sliced
¼ cup lemon juice
1 teaspoon salt
¼ cup oil
1 tablespoon parsley

Toast sesame seeds on flat pan at 350° for 10 minutes or on top of stove, stirring constantly./Put in blender and blend until they become a powdery paste./Add oil and blend for 10 seconds./Drain garbanzos, saving liquid./Add remaining ingredients except parsley and blend./Gradually add enough bean liquid to consistency of thick mashed potatoes./Add parsley./Cover and chill./Serve at room temperature, either as an appetizer or on lettuce with celery and tomato sections./This makes a very good luncheon salad served with a French or Syrian bread and cream soup.

Mrs. George N. Proctor,
Ladies' Committee Associate

Cheese Lace

"Most unusual! Delicious cocktail accompaniment."

Yield: 100 pieces

Extra sharp bar cheese (coon cheese, for example)

Cut cheese into ¼-inch slices, then cut each slice into 9 cubes./Place cubes on Teflon cookie sheet about 2 inches apart./Bake at 350° until they cease to bubble (about 7 minutes)./Remove with spatula, drain on paper towel./Wipe off cookie sheet and repeat./Will keep for several days in airtight container.

Mrs. Henry Brown,
Ladies' Committee Associate

Gail's Delicious Hot Cocktail Dip

"No one can guess how this is made. They think there is crabmeat in it, but there is none."

Yield: 1½ pints

1 (16-ounce) can peeled tomatoes
2 cans whole green chilies
1 medium-large yellow onion, chopped
1 heaping teaspoon Lawry's seasoning salt
1 (8-ounce) package cream cheese

Put tomatoes in saucepan./Add onion to tomatoes./Drain and seed chilies, then chop in small pieces and add to tomatoes and onion./Cook until onion is soft./Add seasoning salt./Turn off heat and add cream cheese./This amount should make the right consistency for dip./If too runny, add more cheese; if too thick add just a bit more tomatoes./Put into chafing dish./Serve hot with taco-flavored chips.

Mrs. Elizabeth P. Gardner,
Ladies' Committee

Taramasalata

"A delicious Greek appetizer."

Yield: about 1 pint

⅓ (8-ounce) jar of Tarama* (carp roe)
1 small onion, finely grated
1 cup olive oil
4 or 5 slices white bread, without crusts
juice of 2-3 lemons

Mash Tarama and add grated onion./Add a little of the oil and beat thoroughly to a smooth paste./Moisten bread with water; squeeze out excess water./Continue beating Tarama mixture, adding alternately small bits of moistened bread, olive oil, and lemon juice./It should be beaten until a very pale orange color./This may be served as a dip with crackers or spread on toast.

Mrs. George D. Mason,
Ladies' Committee Associate

*available at Greek or international groceries

Fort Bliss Chile con Queso

"Served at almost every party in the Southwest, this is still a novelty in New England. A simple version, not too hot."

Serves 8-10

1 medium onion, chopped
1 can taco sauce
½ pound cheese (Monterey Jack or cheddar), grated
evaporated milk

Sauté onion in a little butter or oil./Add taco sauce./Simmer for 5 minutes and add cheese./Heat until cheese melts, adding evaporated milk to smooth the mixture to desired consistency./Serve hot with Fritos or tortilla chips.

Mrs. Marsden P. Earle, Jr.,
Ladies' Committee

Camembert with Nuts

"This mellows and glorifies plain Camembert."
                                            Serves 6-8

¼ cup butter, softened
¼ cup pecans, ground
2 tablespoons lemon juice
Tabasco
1 (8-ounce) wheel Camembert or Brie,
    chilled

Cream butter; blend in nuts, lemon juice, and a
few drops of Tabasco./Cut cheese wheel in half
horizontally while it is cold./Spread bottom
with butter mixture and replace top./Chill
until firm./Remove from refrigerator ½ hour
before serving with crackers or melba toast.

                        Mrs. John A. Kirkpatrick, Jr.,
                        Ladies' Committee

Brie en Croute

"Melting hot Brie in a flaky crust. Delicious!"
                                            Serves 10

2-pound round of Brie
1 package refrigerated crescent-roll mix
1 egg yolk

Place Brie on a round oven-to-table platter./
Roll one package crescent-roll dough ¼-inch
thick./Cover top and sides of Brie, using extra
dough as decorations./Brush entire surface
with egg wash made by mixing an egg yolk
with a teaspoon of water./Prick with a fork./
Bake 15 minutes at 375° until brown./Cut in
wedges and serve immediately.

                        Mrs. John B. Sears,
                        Ladies' Committee

Caution: Do not attempt to bake on a sheet and
move to a platter./Once the Brie bakes, it runs.

Crabmeat Appetizer

"A quickie for the food processor."
                                            Yield: 4 cups

1-1½ cups crabmeat
juice of 1 lemon *or* 3 tablespoons dry
    white wine
Tabasco
2 (8-ounce) packages cream cheese,
    softened
¼ cup mayonnaise
½ cup sour cream
⅛ teaspoon salt
2 teaspoons dry mustard
1 tablespoon minced onion
1 tablespoon confectioner's sugar
1 teaspoon cream-style horseradish

Marinate crabmeat in lemon juice or white
wine and 2-3 dashes Tabasco, for the time it
takes to prepare the rest./If you have a food
processor, whir all the other ingredients in it,
then fold in crabmeat./Otherwise, blend
cream cheese and sour cream until smooth./
Beat in mayonnaise, salt, onion, and
horseradish./Blend together sugar and dry
mustard./Add to cream cheese mixture./Beat
well./Fold in crabmeat./Serve with crackers
or melba toast.

                        Mrs. Richard P. C. Fitzgerald,
                        Ladies' Committee

• Cocktail cookies are always on hand if you
  mix ½ cup flour with ½ cup butter and 1 jar
  of bacon-cheese spread. Shape into a roll
  and keep in the refrigerator or freezer. Then
  slice thinly as needed and bake at 450° for
  10 minutes.

• Red caviar swirled into cream cheese softened with sour cream is delicious on crisp
  melba toast.

Smoked Oysters en Croute

"A delicious appetizer brought from Hawaii."

Serves 8-10

1 can smoked oysters
1 can refrigerator or flake rolls

Drain oysters./Separate rolls into flakes, using one flake or layer for each oyster./Place oyster in center of flake and wrap dough around, sealing carefully./Place on greased baking sheet./ Bake at 375° for about 8 minutes or until dough is browned./May be prepared early in the day and refrigerated until ready for baking.

Mrs. Shattuck W. Osborne,
Ladies' Committee Associate

Ramon Novarro's Guacamole

"It is said that Novarro could exist on this guacamole for weeks, a tempting idea."

Yield: 3 cups

2 avocados
½ can green chili (about 3 tablespoons)
½ pound seedless grapes
½ teaspoon salt
2 tablespoons oil
2 tablespoons vinegar

Peel avocados and mash./Wash the green chili well and chop, adding it to the avocados./ Season with salt, vinegar, and olive oil to taste./Add grapes to the mixture. (Instead of grapes, Novarro added pomegranate seeds, which give a very colorful appearance.)

Deac Rossell, Film Coordinator,
Public Education

• **Dunk cubes of veal sausage in a mixture of sour cream and chives, or sour cream and dill, or sour cream and caraway.**

Caviar Mousse

"It disappears at a party."

Serves 20-30

9 hard-cooked eggs
1½ envelopes unflavored gelatin
3 tablespoons lemon juice
3 tablespoons dry vermouth
1½ cups mayonnaise
1½ teaspoons Sauce Diable
1 tablespoon onion, minced
2 (3¼-ounce) jars lumpfish caviar

Lightly oil a 4-cup mold./Rice or chop eggs./ Place in a large mixing bowl./Dissolve gelatin in lemon juice and vermouth in top of double boiler./Add mayonnaise, sauce, and onion to eggs./Fold in gelatin, blending carefully./Fold in caviar./Pour into mold and chill./Unmold and serve with pumpernickel or rusk-type cracker.

Mrs. Mayo A. Shattuck,
Ladies' Committee Associate

Spinach Balls

"This I picked up at a very happy hour on Siesta Key, Florida."

Yield: 50-60

1 package frozen chopped spinach, thawed
1½ cups Pepperidge Farm poultry stuffing
3 eggs
1 tablespoon dill weed

Mix all ingredients together./Let stand for about 10 minutes so crumbs become moist./ Shape into small balls, place on cookie sheet and freeze./Store in plastic bag in freezer./ Bake on cookie sheet at 350° for ½-¾ hour.

Mrs. George Marks,
Ladies' Committee Associate

Cheese Hors d'Oeuvre

"Keep a batch in the freezer for quick hors d'oeuvre."

Yield: 50-70

6 English muffins, split
10 ounces cheddar cheese, grated
½ cup black olives, chopped
2 small onions, finely chopped
¼ teaspoon curry powder
2 tablespoons mayonnaise
paprika

Split and toast English muffins./Mix cheddar cheese, black olives, onion, mayonnaise, and curry./Spread on English muffins./Sprinkle paprika on top./Cut muffins in quarters with kitchen scissors. (At this point you can freeze, then defrost and heat in oven until bubbly.)/ Bake at 350° about 7 minutes.

Mrs. Irving H. Chase,
Ladies' Committee Associate

Cocktail Cheese Crackers

"Lightly sharp, with a 'more please' flavor."
Yield: 50 crackers

2 cups sharp cheddar cheese, grated
½ pound butter, softened
½ teaspoon cayenne
2 cups Rice Krispies
2 cups flour

Use your fingers to mix all together./Form into small balls, size of walnut./Place on ungreased Teflon cookie sheet and press down with tines of a fork./Bake at 350° for 12-15 minutes./Store in an airtight container. (These freeze well too.)

Mrs. Lester A. Steinberg, Ladies' Committee

Herbed Cheese

"Why buy Boursin when you can make your own."

Yield: ½ pint

8 ounces cream cheese
1 or 2 cloves garlic
1 teaspoon *each* (all dried):
caraway seed
basil
dill weed
chives
parsley

Blend well in food processor, using steel blade./Pack into small bowl, dusting with freshly ground black pepper. (Best made a day ahead and refrigerated.)

Mrs. Henry F. Cate, Jr.,
Ladies' Committee Associate

Mystery Morsels

"A quick and easy bite that everyone likes."
Yield: 36

12 slices white bread
chunky peanut butter
12 slices lean bacon

Make 6 peanut butter sandwiches./Trim crusts, cut sandwiches into thirds, then each third in half./Cut each bacon strip into thirds and wrap a piece around mini-sandwich, securing with a toothpick./Bake on the rack of a drip pan at 400° until the bacon is crisp.

Mrs. Malcom L. Trayser,
Ladies' Committee Associate

• Mix 2 tablespoons Parmesan cheese with 2 tablespoons buttered crumbs, 1 teaspoon basil, and ¼ teaspoon onion salt. Dip halved cherry tomatoes in the mixture and broil (coated side up) until top browns. Do not allow tomatoes to become soft.

Crudités Différents

"An attractive and unusual way of serving crudités."

Yield: 4 cups

endive
fresh edible-pod peas
Dip
1 package chopped frozen spinach, thawed
   and squeezed dry
1 cup mayonnaise
1 cup sour cream
½ cup scallion tops, minced in processor
¼ cup parsley, minced in processor
¼ teaspoon dried dill weed
½ teaspoon Jane's Crazy Salt
¼ teaspoon pepper, freshly ground
1 tablespoon fresh lemon juice

Separate endive into individual leaves./Cut ends off peas and leave whole./Mix dip. (Process and chill a day ahead to blend.)/Fill glass bowl with dip deep enough for endive and peas to stand upright around it.

Mrs. William C. Haskins,
Ladies' Committee

Petite Quiche Hors d'Oeuvres

"These may be frozen and reheated in slow oven for 15 minutes."

Yield: 24 petite quiches

¼ pound margarine
2 ounces cream cheese
1 cup flour
2 tablespoons margarine
1 large onion, chopped
2 ounces Swiss cheese
2 eggs
½ cup milk
¼ teaspoon pepper
nutmeg

In a mixer or food processor mix margarine, cream cheese, and flour./Form into a ball and refrigerate until firm./Divide into 24 balls./ Press into miniature cupcake tins and refrigerate overnight./In 2 tablespoons margarine, sauté onion until golden./Evenly distribute cooked onion and grated cheese in individual pastries./Beat together eggs, milk, pepper, and nutmeg and pour into cheese-filled pastries./ Bake at 400° 15 minutes, then reduce temperature to 300° and bake 15 minutes more.

Mrs. Lester A. Steinberg,
Ladies' Committee

Parsley "Pesto" with Carrots

"These are the ingredients for pesto but parsley is substituted for basil and the mixture is served as a "dip" with raw carrots. Absolutely delicious!"

Yield: about 2 cups

1 bunch Italian flat-leaf parsley
3 cloves garlic, crushed
olive oil
Parmesan cheese, freshly grated
salt and pepper, freshly ground
½ cup walnuts, chopped

In a food processor, using the steel blade, chop parsley fine./Add the garlic and slowly pour in olive oil until the mixture is moist./Stir in the Parmesan cheese (begin with ½ cup and add more according to taste)./Season with salt and pepper./Stir in the walnuts and refrigerate overnight to allow the flavors to blend. (Freezes well.)/Serve with carrots cut flat and wide so that it is easier to scoop up the "dip."/ Or spread on carrots with a knife.

Miss Ellen Stillman,
Ladies' Committee Associate

Fried Squid

"Squid is easily prepared and a delightful novelty at the cocktail hour. Guests have welcomed this unusual tidbit."

Serves 6

2 pounds fresh squid
salt and pepper
flour

Clean, skin, and wash squid thoroughly, removing ink sac, eye, and cartilage, and cut into desired size./Dry well with paper towels./Lightly sprinkle with salt and pepper, then dredge with flour./Put ½ inch of good olive oil into skillet and when very hot fry the squid (without crowding the pan) and cook until golden brown./Remove from pan and drain on paper towel./Sprinkle with salt and pepper as desired.

This may be served as a first course or as an hors d'oeuvre with cocktails./It may be fried early in the day and put under broiler to crisp when served.

Mrs. Augustine Bombaci,
Ladies' Committee Associate

Marinade of Little Squid

"Tiny squid are hard to find but are exceedingly tantalizing as a first course."

Serves 4-6

2 pounds of *little* squid
8 tablespoons olive oil
3 teaspoons wine vinegar
1 fresh lemon

Clean the squid thoroughly, cut into medium-size pieces, and simmer gently for about 8 minutes./Drain and set aside./Make dressing of oil, vinegar, juice of lemon, and salt to taste./Lemon rind, finely stripped, may be added to marinade for taste and color./Pour dressing over squid and marinate for several hours./Serve very cold on a bed of tender young chicory leaves.

One of the following may be added for variety:
fresh little necks, steamed
fresh mussels, steamed
fresh scallops, tenderly poached
fresh tiny shrimp, poached

Mrs. Augustine Bombaci,
Ladies' Committee Associate

Steak on a Stick or Beef Teriyaki

"An excellent, different hors d'oeuvre, very easy to make."

Yield: 8 pieces

1 pound flank steak

Meat Marinade
3 tablespoons light soy sauce
3 tablespoons dark soy sauce
2 tablespoons sugar
4 tablespoons sherry
3 cloves garlic, minced
1 wedge fresh ginger (about the size of
  a silver dollar), minced
4 tablespoons sesame oil

Mix the meat marinade ingredients well./Unroll the entire flank steak, trim off the fat and cut into 1-inch slices across the grain./Marinate the meat at least 4 hours, then string the sliced meat on bamboo skewers* like ribbon candy./Barbecue over charcoal or in the broiler./Brown 4 inches away from the broiler for just a few minutes, turning over once to brown both sides.

Mrs. George A. Schlichte,
Ladies' Committee Associate

*The bamboo skewers can be purchased in Chinatown shops or in restaurant supply houses.

Shrimp Toast

"Don't be tempted to purée the shrimp in the food processor; it is worth the effort to chop them by hand and you will pleased with the resultant texture."

Yield: 24 pieces

6 slices thin, dry white bread
½ pound fresh shrimp
2 tablespoons fresh pork fat
8 water chestnuts
2 stalks scallions, including the green ends, chopped fine
1 teaspoon salt
2 tablespoons sherry
1½ tablespoons cornstarch
1 egg, lightly beaten
sesame seeds
paprika
about 4 cups of oil for deep frying

Trim bread of crusts./Cut each slice into 4 squares or triangles./Shell, devein, and clean shrimp./Chop the shrimp very finely into a pulp-like paste./Chop pork fat and water chestnuts until fine./Mix well with shrimp, scallions, salt, sherry, cornstarch, and beaten egg./Spread mixture on the bread pieces./Sprinkle sesame seeds and paprika on the filling and press lightly so they adhere to the mixture./Heat the oil to 375° or until it is very hot, but not smoking./Drop bread, shrimp side down, into oil and fry for about 30 seconds./Turn and fry on the other side for another 30 seconds./Both sides should be golden./Drain on paper towels and serve hot.

If you wish to prepare the shrimp toast ahead of time and freeze, deep fry the bread and mixture until it becomes a light beige, cool, and freeze./To reheat, preheat oven to 350°, place frozen toast in a single layer on a cookie sheet, and heat for 10-12 minutes./The shrimp toast will become more golden as it is reheated.

Mrs. George A. Schlichte,
Ladies' Committee Associate

Hot Cheese Appetizer

"What could be more simple, more delicious?"

1 cup Hellmann's mayonnaise
8 ounces sharp Cracker Barrel cheese, grated
1 small onion, grated

Mix together in small oven-proof dish./Bake at 300° for 15 minutes./Serve hot with crisp crackers or melba toast.

Mrs. R. Willis Leith, Jr.,
Ladies' Committee

Gougère

"A hearty hors d'oeuvre or luncheon dish, good with soup or salad. We have it for brunch on Christmas Day."

Serves 4-8

1 cup water
6 tablespoons butter
1 teaspoon salt
⅛ teaspoon pepper
1 cup sifted flour
4 eggs
1 cup Gruyère or good Swiss cheese, grated

Preheat oven to 425°./Use round Teflon baking sheet, or any cookie sheet, lightly greased./Put butter, water, salt, and pepper in saucepan./Heat until butter is melted and mixture boils rapidly./Add flour all at once./Cook, stirring until mixture forms a ball./Remove from heat./Beat in eggs, one at a time, incorporating each before adding next./Stir in all but 2 tablespoons cheese./Place rounded tablespoons of dough on baking sheet to form a ring./Sprinkle with remaining cheese./Bake 40-45 minutes until puffed and brown.

Mrs. Marsden P. Earle, Jr.,
Ladies' Committee

Chef's Jalapeño Dip

"For raw vegetables, fried fish, shrimp, or cold meats."

Yield: about 1 pint

1 whole head of garlic, mashed
2 ends of dry bread
2 Jalapeño peppers and juice
6 ripe tomatoes
2 peppers
1 peeled cucumber
1 tablespoon paprika
2 tablespoons vinegar
2 tablespoons olive oil
½ cup skinless almonds, chopped

Put all items except the almonds through a grinder, fine blade, or whir in a food processor./Add almonds and salt to taste.

Chef Alfred Georgs,
Museum Restaurant

Smoked Oyster Spread

"Different and so easy to make. Freezes well."

Yield: 1 pint

1 sardine-size can smoked oysters
1 (8-ounce) package cream cheese, softened
1 small can ripe olives, drained and
  chopped

If the smoked oysters are packed in cottonseed oil, pour it off as it contains much of the smoked taste./Chop the oysters./Mix with cream cheese and olives./Refrigerate./Serve on crackers or melba toast. (Mayonnaise may be added if you want a softer spread.)

Mrs. Claude E. Welch,
Ladies' Committee Associate

Eggs à la Polonaise

"I serve the eggs sometimes to start a dinner, sometimes for lunch with asparagus, broccoli, or salad and always with French bread. Smacznego! (bon appetit).

Serves 8

12 hard-cooked eggs
shallots or minced onions, sautéed in butter
fresh or dry dill weed
fresh parsley, chopped
salt and pepper
white bread crumbs
butter or margarine

With a sharp knife cut the eggs lengthwise in half./Remove egg gently with spoon, leaving the eggshells intact./Chop the eggs very finely./Add generously of the sautéed chopped onions, dill, and parsley; salt and pepper to taste./Mix well but gently./Fill the empty egg shells with the mixture, without packing them too tightly./Dip the filled portion of eggs in bread crumbs and sauté on low heat for 15 minutes./Serve hot.

Mrs. E. Anthony Kutten,
Museum Art Tour Coordinator

- On toothpicks, spear ham cubes and sweet-sour onions; roll in Parmesan cheese.

- Wrap smoked oysters in partially cooked bacon; bake at 450° until bacon is crisp.

- Soak peels of potatoes in salted water for one hour in the refrigerator. Pat dry. Spread with melted butter, bake at 400° until crisp. Sprinkle with more salt if needed (and with chopped parsley for color).

Artichoke Heart Elégant

"Every time I serve this people ask for the recipe."

Yield: 50-60 pieces

4 (6-ounce) jars artichokes in oil
2 small onions, chopped
1½ cloves garlic, chopped or minced
8 eggs, beaten
½ cup saltine cracker crumbs
¼ teaspoon oregano
½ teaspoon salt
¼ teaspoon pepper
¼ teaspoon Tabasco
4 cups shredded cheddar cheese (1 pound)
2 teaspoons parsley, minced

Drain oil of 2 jars artichokes into skillet./Add garlic and onions; cook until tender (discard oil of remaining 2 jars of artichokes)./Beat eggs./Add all ingredients and mix./Bake 30-40 minutes at 325° in 9 x 13-inch pan./Let stand 10 minutes before cutting./Serve as a luncheon dish or bite-size *hors d'oeuvres.* (May be frozen or made one or two days before and heated.)

Mrs. Anthony J. Medaglia, Jr.,
Ladies' Committee Associate

- Boil tiny new potatoes, jackets on. Scoop out a bit of the center and top with sour cream, chives, and crisp bacon bits. (If you really want to splurge, fill them with sour cream and caviar.)

- Spread salami slices with chutney and broil.

- Make your own melba toast: trim crusts from thin-sliced bread, cut in half, bake at 325° until lightly golden.

Saucisson Enveloppé

"If we don't serve this variation of Pigs-in-Blankets at a party guests ask why."

Yield: 40

1 can refrigerated biscuits
1 box frozen brown-and-serve sausage

Separate biscuits and cut in fourths and flatten slightly with palm of hand./Cut each link sausage in 7 pieces./Wrap ¼ of biscuit around sausage and pinch folds./Place on greased cookie sheet, fold side down./Brush tops with melted butter./Bake 12-14 minutes at 400° until golden./Serve on hot tray.

(Can be prepared several hours ahead and refrigerated until ready to bake.)

Mrs. William C. Haskins,
Ladies' Committee Associate

- Spoon into crisp endive leaves a mixture of cream cheese and lemon juice topped with red caviar.

- Core slim cucumbers; stuff with a mixture of cream cheese, Worcestershire, garlic salt, and herbs. Chill, slice, and serve on pumpernickel or rye toast.

- Heat a can of condensed black bean soup in a chafing dish; stir in grated cheddar cheese, tomato sauce, and bourbon. Serve warm with corn chips.

- A perfect marriage of flavors is tiny white cauliflower flowerettes served with Durkee's Dressing as a dip. People will say "Mmmm...how did you make this?"

- Wrap half-slices of bacon around large walnut halves. Fasten with toothpicks. Bake on a rack at 400° about 15 minutes, turning once.

EGYPTIAN (Giza, 5th Dynasty, Old Kingdom)
Statuette of a woman grinding corn. Limestone
Harvard-Boston Expedition

Breads & Muffins

Trade Wind Muffins

"From my Michigan daughter."

Yield: 24

1 (20-ounce) can crushed pineapple
½ cup slivered almonds
2 cups sifted all-purpose flour
1 teaspoon baking soda
1 teaspoon salt
1 (3-ounce) package cream cheese, softened
1 cup sugar
2 teaspoons vanilla
1 large egg, beaten
½ cup sour cream

Drain pineapple thoroughly, reserve syrup./
Heavily grease muffin pans; sprinkle with
almonds./Resift flour with soda and salt./Beat
cheese, sugar, and vanilla together until
smooth, blend in egg./Add flour mixture alternately with sour cream./Fold in drained
pineapple./Spoon into prepared muffin pans
and bake at 350° for 35 minutes or until muffins are golden brown and test done./Remove
from oven and let stand in pans 5-10 minutes,
then turn out onto wire rack and spread with
following glaze:

1 tablespoon soft margarine
1 cup 4-X sugar, sifted
1 tablespoon syrup from pineapple

Mrs. John H. Halford, Jr.,
Ladies' Committee Associate

Molasses Muffins

"A specialty of the house. Unusually good."

Yield: 2 dozen

¾ cup butter or margarine
1 cup sugar
3 eggs
½ cup molasses
3 cups cake flour
¾ teaspoon salt
2 teaspoons baking powder
¾ teaspoon baking soda
¾ cup buttermilk

Cream the shortening and sugar./Beat in the
eggs, one at a time./Add the molasses./Sift the
dry ingredients, and add alternately with the
buttermilk./Pour into 24 buttered and floured
muffin tins./Bake at 375° for 20 minutes.
(These are best split and toasted under the
broiler. They also freeze well.)

Miss Ellen Stillman,
Ladies' Committee Associate

Beta Challah

"Braided loaves made with beet broth for a
beautiful light rosy color."

Yield: 4 loaves

3 cups warm beet broth
2 tablespoons yeast
2½ teaspoons salt
⅓ cup honey
½ cup butter, melted
4 eggs, beaten
7-9 cups whole-wheat flour
sesame seeds

Dissolve yeast in broth; proof for 10 minutes./
Add salt, honey, butter, and eggs, reserving 2
tablespoons of the eggs./Mix in 3 cups flour
and beat until dough begins to become elastic;
then add remaining flour and knead for 10 or
15 minutes./Allow to rise for 1 hour in warm
place./Punch down./Divide into 4 sections
and make 3 "ropes" out of each section, braid-
ing the "ropes" into 14-inch loaves./Allow to
rise on baking sheets for ½ hour./Brush with
egg and sprinkle with sesame seeds./Bake at
350° for 30 minutes.

Judy Spear, Editor, Publications

CAMILLE PISSARRO (French, 1831–1903)
Market at Pontoise. Gouache with watercolor. M. and M. Karolik Fund

Sour-Cream Johnny Cake

"A favorite recipe for 20 years."

Serves 8

¾ cup stone-ground corn meal
¾ cup flour
¼ cup sugar (or less)
½ teaspoon salt
3 teaspoons baking powder
¼ teaspoon baking soda
1 egg, beaten
1 cup sour cream

Mix and sift dry ingredients./Add egg and sour cream./Beat to a smooth batter./Bake in a well-buttered pan at 400° for about 25 minutes.

Miss Elizabeth Storer,
Ladies' Committee Associate

Oatmeal-Raisin Bread

"No kneading, no rising for this delicious bread."

Yield: 1 loaf

1 cup rolled oats
1 cup buttermilk
½ cup dark brown sugar, firmly packed
1 extra large egg, well beaten
1 cup whole-wheat flour
1 teaspoon baking powder
½ teaspoon baking soda
1 teaspoon salt
6 tablespoons butter, melted
3 tablespoons wheat germ
1 cup yellow raisins (or half raisins,
   half nuts)

In a large bowl, soak rolled oats in buttermilk 45 minutes to 1 hour./Stir in sugar and egg./Add all the other ingredients./Mix thoroughly./Bake in a buttered bread pan about 40 minutes at 400°.

Miss Ellen Stillman,
Ladies' Committee Associate

Whole-Wheat Bread

"The only bread I know made entirely of whole-wheat flour and yet not heavy."

Yield: 3 loaves

3 envelopes dry yeast
¾ cup lukewarm water
pinch of sugar
3 cups lukewarm milk
6 tablespoons butter
⅓ cup dark brown sugar, packed
¼ cup molasses
3 tablespoons wheat germ
3 tablespoons toasted sesame seeds
2 eggs, lightly beaten
1 tablespoon salt
9 cups stone-ground whole-wheat flour

In a small bowl, proof the yeast in lukewarm water and sugar for 10 minutes./In large bowl, combine the milk, butter, brown sugar, molasses, wheat germ, and sesame seeds./Stir in the eggs, the yeast mixture, and 3 cups of flour./Stir until smooth./Cover with towel and let stand in warm place 25 minutes.

Beat in 4 cups of flour, 1 cup at a time./Turn dough out on a floured surface, and knead in 2 more cups of flour./Continue kneading until dough is smooth and elastic./Form into a ball./Place in a large buttered bowl, brush top with melted butter./Cover with a towel and let rise in a warm place about 1 hour or until double in bulk./Punch down./Divide into 3 buttered loaf pans./Let rise, covered, in warm place 30 minutes or until dough reaches tops of pans.

Brush with beaten egg./Bake at 350° for 45 minutes or until tops are browned and bottoms sound hollow when tapped.

Miss Ellen Stillman,
Ladies' Committee Associate

EDOUARD VUILLARD (French, 1868–1940)
The Cook, 1899. Color lithograph. Bequest of W.G. Russell Allen

Blueberry Muffins

"A treasured recipe from Vermont, and good enough for dessert!"

Yield: 6 large or 8 medium muffins

½ cup butter(not margarine)
¾ cup sugar
2 eggs
2 cups flour
2 teaspoons baking powder
½ teaspoon salt
½ cup milk
1 cup blueberries

Cream butter and sugar well./Stir in eggs one at a time./Combine and add dry ingredients./Stir in milk, small amount at at time./Fold in blueberries./Spoon batter into 6 large or 8 medium-size muffin cups and bake for 30 minutes at 375°.

Mrs. Robert L. M. Ahern,
Ladies' Committee Associate

Maple Muffins

"So simple, so good!"

Yield: 12 medium-size muffins

¼ cup milk
1 egg, slightly beaten
1¾ cups flour
2½ teaspoons baking powder
¼ teaspoon salt
1 cup *real* maple syrup
¼ cup melted butter

Whip milk into beaten egg./Sift together flour, baking powder, and salt./Add to egg-milk mixture a little at a time, alternating with maple syrup./Fold in melted butter./Pour into greased muffin tins./Bake at 325° for 25 minutes.

Mrs. Richard P. C. Fitzgerald,
Ladies' Committee

Ecology Bread

"This recipe, given to me by a friend, makes our favorite oatmeal bread. We enjoy it for breakfast, toasted, with homemade rhubarb or strawberry jam."

Yield: 2 loaves

1 cup water
1 cup milk
¼ cup peanut or salad oil
1 cup rolled oats
2 teaspoons salt
½ cup molasses
1 package dry yeast
4½ – 5½ cups King Arthur white flour

Combine water, milk, and oil in saucepan and bring to a boil./Shut off heat; add rolled oats and stir./Cool to lukewarm./Pour into mixer bowl; add salt, molasses, and yeast./Beat 2 minutes at medium speed./Lower speed and add flour gradually until dough no longer sticks to sides of the bowl./Knead for 10 minutes with dough hook attachment, or by hand on floured board. (James Beard does both, and I find it makes a finer textured bread)./Place dough in buttered bowl, turning dough to grease top./Cover with towel and let rise in warm place until double in bulk./Punch down, divide in half, form loaves and place in 2 buttered heavy, standard-size bread pans./Let rise until double in bulk./Bake at 375° for 35-40 minutes, or until the loaves sound hollow when tapped.

Mrs. Robert L. M. Ahern,
Ladies' Committee Associate

Honey-Oatmeal Bread

"A delicious easy-to-make bread."

Yield: 2 loaves

1 cup water
1 cup milk
4 tablespoons butter
1 cup rolled oats
½ cup honey
2 packages dry yeast
1 teaspoon salt
4-5 cups unbleached white flour

Combine liquids and butter and heat until boiling./Off heat, add oatmeal and cool to lukewarm./Transfer to large mixing bowl, add honey and yeast, and beat hard for 2-3 minutes./Add salt and gradually beat in flour until dough can be handled./Knead on floured board for 8 minutes, adding flour only as needed./Let rise in greased bowl, covered with a clean towel, until doubled./Punch down./Divide in half./Place in 2 greased bread pans./Let rise again until doubled./Bake at 375° about 35-40 minutes or until lightly brown and sounds "hollow" when you knock it with your knuckles.

Mrs. Selwyn A. Kudisch,
Ladies' Committee

▪ *"Hospitality is a little fire, a little food, and immense quiet."*

Ralph Waldo Emerson

▪ *"The discovery of a new dish does more for the happiness of mankind than the discovery of a new star."*

Brillat-Savarin

"Six Weeks" Bran Muffins

"Store the dough in the refrigerator up to six weeks and bake as needed (do not freeze dough). My mother gave me the recipe, and family and guests have enjoyed it for years."

Yield: about 4 dozen

4 eggs
3 cups sugar
1 cup oil
5 cups sifted flour
2 teaspoons salt
1 quart buttermilk
1 (15-ounce) box bran cereal with raisins

Beat eggs; add sugar and oil./Beat well./Add sifted dry ingredients alternately with buttermilk./Mix in cereal./Bake at 400° in muffin tins for 10-20 minutes (depending on size of tin).

Mrs. Mayo A. Shattuck,
Ladies' Committee Associate

▪ **"Of all the books produced since the most remote ages by human talents and industry, those only that treat of cooking are, from a moral point of view, above suspicion. The intention of every other piece of prose may be discussed and even mistrusted, but the purpose of a cookery book is one and unmistakable. Its object can conceivably be no other than to increase the happiness of mankind."**

Joseph Conrad

Breakfast, Brunch & Lunch

Ruffly Pancake

"This billows and ruffles, never the same shape twice."

Serves 2

3 eggs
½ cup flour
¼ teaspoon salt
2 tablespoons sugar
½ cup milk
2 tablespoons butter, melted

Butter a heavy 10-inch skillet (one with an oven-proof handle)./Beat the eggs until fluffy./Stir in the remaining ingredients./Pour the batter into a cold skillet./Place the skillet in a 450° oven./Bake exactly 18 minutes./Turn the oven down to 350°./Bake 10 minutes longer./The pancake will billow up on the sides and be depressed in the center./For a Sunday brunch, serve it with Canadian bacon and apple slices cooked in butter and brown sugar until just tender and glazed./Or for dessert, serve the pancake sprinkled with lemon juice and dusted with powdered sugar./To gild the lily, sweetened strawberries may be added.

Miss Ellen Stillman,
Ladies' Committee Associate

Johnson's Rolled Pancakes

"Roll this pancake as you would a crepe. Enjoy!"

Serves 8 or more

5 eggs
1 cup flour
1½ cups milk
½ teaspoon salt

Beat eggs until well mixed./Add flour and salt and mix well./Gradually add milk and beat until smooth./Batter will be thin.

Heat grill or skillet until very hot./Add 1 teaspoon vegetable oil./Cover grill with very thin layer of batter./Brown on both sides.

Suggested toppings:
sour cream topped with strawberries or
**   blueberries**
sour cream sprinkled with granulated sugar
butter and brown sugar
butter and maple syrup
any combination of above

Howard W. Johnson, Trustee

Old-Fashioned Buckwheat Cakes

"A Philadelphia recipe."

Yield: 15-18

⅓ cup fine yellow corn meal
2 cups milk, scalded
⅓ teaspoon salt
¼ yeast cake, dissolved in ½ cup lukewarm
**   water**
1¼ cups buckwheat flour
1 tablespoon Barbados molasses
¼ teaspoon baking soda, dissolved in ¼ cup
**   lukewarm water**

Pour milk over corn meal and soak ½ hour./Add salt, dissolved yeast, and buckwheat to make the batter thin enough to pour./Let rise overnight./In the morning stir well, adding molasses, baking soda, and water./Pour on hot buttered griddle one at a time.

Mrs. J. Wallace McMeel,
Ladies' Committee Associate

• **Hot applesauce and yogurt is a good pancake topping.**

Sautéed Chicken Livers Georgs' Style

"A popular luncheon dish at the Museum Restaurant."

Serves 4-6

4 strips of bacon, cut into ½-inch squares
1 onion, diced
1 pound fresh chicken livers, large diced
2 apples, seeds removed, sliced thin, then cut into ½-inch pieces
½ teaspoon good curry powder
1½ ounces soy sauce
½ cup cold water
1 tablespoon cornstarch
fresh parsley, chopped

Sauté the bacon with additional drop of fat./ When rendered, add the onions, then the chicken livers./Do not overcook the livers./ When still pink, add the apple and season with curry./Add soy sauce to water and stir in the cornstarch./Pour liquid over the mixture in the pan./If it becomes too thick, add additional water./Garnish with parsley.

Chef Alfred Georgs,
Museum Restaurant

Zucchini Soufflé

"Prepare the ingredients ahead, then assemble quickly for a delicious luncheon dish."

Serves 6-8

8-10 slices bacon
3-4 medium onions, chopped
3 medium zucchini, sliced
1½ cups cheddar cheese, grated
1 (8-ounce) cup sour cream
2 eggs, separated
¼ teaspoon cream of tartar
3 tablespoons flour
¾ cup bread crumbs, tossed with a little bacon fat or melted butter

Cook the bacon until crisp./Drain on paper towels./In some of the bacon fat, cook the onions until limp and slightly colored./Steam the zucchini 5 minutes and cool./In a bowl, mix the sour cream, egg yolks, and flour./In another bowl, beat the egg whites with cream of tartar until stiff./Fold into sour cream mixture.

To assemble, butter a soufflé dish, arrange in layers half of each: zucchini, sour cream mixture, crumbled bacon, onions, and cheese./ Repeat layers./Top with buttered crumbs./ Bake at 350° for 25-30 minutes or until crumbs are golden brown.

Barbara Lambert,
Keeper of Musical Instruments

Ham and Cheese Soufflé

"A favorite at the Museum Restaurant."

Serves 4

6 tablespoons flour
2¼ cups light cream
4 eggs, separated
3 ounces ham, diced
6 ounces Swiss cheese, grated
salt

Preheat oven to 375°./Whisk the flour into the light cream./Bring to a boil, stirring constantly./Cool./Add egg yolks, ham, and cheese to the thickened cream./Season to taste./Beat egg whites until stiff but not dry./ Fold whites into cheese mixture./Pour into a well-greased oven-proof dish./Bake at 375° for 30-40 minutes.

Chef Alfred Georgs,
Museum Restaurant

• **⅓ cup butter, ⅓ cup sugar, and ½ can frozen orange juice concentrate, heated to dissolve the sugar, makes a delicious orange syrup for pancakes or waffles.**

PAUL OUTERBRIDGE, JR. (American, 1896–1958)
Semi-abstraction of eggs in a bowl, 1922. Photograph
Gift of Thea Cottone

Scallop Mousse

"Easy with food processor. May be used for a buffet or lunch."

Serves 20 at cocktails

1 pound deep-sea scallops, side muscles
  removed
3 tablespoons lemon juice
5 egg whites
3 cups heavy cream
salt and white pepper
1 pound small fillets of sole
½ pound salmon
Tabasco
fresh dill or tarragon

Using food processor, blend scallops, adding 1 tablespoon lemon juice, 2 egg whites, then 1 cup heavy cream, salt and pepper./ Refrigerate./Process carefully cleaned sole, adding 2 egg whites and 1 cup heavy cream, salt and pepper, and 1 tablespoon lemon juice./Mix thoroughly in processor or mixer with scallop mixture./Spread half the mixture in well-buttered loaf pan or mold, leaving a trough in center./Refrigerate./Process salmon, 1 egg white, 1 cup cream, remaining lemon juice, salt and pepper, and a drop or two of Tabasco./Pat into center trough of fish mold./ Cover with remaining half of scallop-fish mixture./Cover with sprigs of fresh dill or tarragon, then buttered foil or paper./Set mold in dish of boiling water and bake at 325° for 35-45 minutes./It will be firm to touch when done and mixture will pull from sides of pan as it cools./Unmold to serve on platter with chilled cooked shrimp, artichoke quarters, and blanched Chinese peapods as garnish./Serve with salad for luncheon or on sliced whole-wheat bread for cocktails.

Mrs. James H. Cannon,
Ladies' Committee Associate

Spanakopeta

"This is a super light lunch. Can be made weeks in advance and popped into the oven. Serve with a tossed green salad."

Yield: 14-16 triangles

2 packages frozen chopped spinach
1 bunch scallions, minced
1 tablespoon dried dill
½ pound feta cheese, crumbled
4 eggs
1 teaspoon salt
¼ teaspoon pepper
4-5 phyllo leaves
3 tablespoons olive oil
¼ pound unsalted butter, melted
sesame seeds, toasted

Cook spinach and drain thoroughly./Sauté in olive oil with scallions and dill, removing additional moisture in the spinach./Remove from heat./Add the feta cheese, eggs, salt, and pepper and blend well./Cut the phyllo leaves into 4-inch strips./It is best to work with one at a time and keep the other leaves covered with a lightly dampened dish towel, since they dry out quickly./With a pastry brush, brush each 4-inch strip with butter./Place 1 heaping table-spoon of the mixture on one corner of each strip and fold to form a triangle, making sure mixture is well distributed into the 3 corners./ Continue folding, as you would a flag, until you have used up the entire strip.Place on a cookie sheet, butter the top of the triangle, sprinkle with sesame seeds, and freeze./Bake frozen at 350° for 30 minutes or until golden brown./For luncheon, serve 2 per person./A smaller version of the above can be made for *hors d'oeuvres,* using strips cut 2 inches wide./ It takes time but the raves will be plentiful./ Freeze and bake at 350° for about 20 minutes.

Mrs. Malcolm L. Trayser,
Ladies' Committee Associate

Crab Casserole

"Equally good for lunch or dinner with rice and a salad."

Serves 4

1 (1-pound) can artichoke hearts
¾ pound fresh crabmeat (or lobster meat)
¼ pound fresh mushrooms, sliced
2 tablespoons butter
1 tablespoon Worcestershire sauce
¼ cup dry sherry
1½ cups medium cream sauce, well
    seasoned
¼ cup mixture of softened bread crumbs
    and Parmesan cheese
paprika

Drain artichoke hearts, arrange in buttered shallow baking dish./Sprinkle crabmeat over them./Sauté mushrooms in butter for 5 minutes and arrange over crabmeat./Add Worcestershire sauce and sherry to white sauce and pour over contents of baking dish./Sprinkle top with crumbs and cheese./Put paprika on top and bake at 375° for 20 minutes./Chopped parsley may be added before serving.

Mrs. Albion C. Drinkwater,
Ladies' Committee Associate

Egg Foo Yong

"This is a good brunch, luncheon, or simple supper dish. The recipe can be varied infinitely by substitution of everything except eggs. Just be sure that the ingredients are shredded in order to bind the omelette."

Serves 6-8

3 strips bacon, cut in thin strips
½ cup cooked shrimp
½ cup barbecued pork (or cooked ham or
    chicken), diced
½ cup bean sprouts
1 small can sliced button mushrooms
2 stalks scallions, including the green ends,
    chopped fine
6 eggs, lightly beaten
¼ teaspoon salt
vegetable or peanut oil for stir-frying

Stir-fry bacon with shrimp and barbecued pork and set aside./Add 1 tablespoon oil to pan and reheat pan./Stir-fry bean sprouts for 1 minute and set aside./Mix bean sprouts, mushrooms, scallions, shrimp, and pork into beaten egg./Pour a little oil into frying pan over medium-high heat./Using ladle, take a scoop of the egg mixture and gently put into the frying pan./Brown on both sides and transfer from frying pan onto paper-lined platter (paper towels will absorb excess oil)./Put platter into preheated oven to keep warm until all the egg mixture is used.

Sauce
1½ cups chicken broth
pinch of salt
½ teaspoon sugar
2 teaspoons dark soy sauce
1 tablespoon cornstarch
2 tablespoons water

Heat sauce mixture in a small pan over medium-high heat./Bring to a boil slowly with frequent stirring./When sauce has thickened, turn heat to very low to keep it warm until ready to use.

Mrs. George A. Schlichte,
Ladies' Committee Associate

Note: To make the omelettes a uniform size, use an omelette pan or cooking rings./Set rings into frying pan and pour egg mixture inside; remove rings when you are ready to brown the other side./I have made cooking rings by cutting a 1-pound coffee can into 1-inch rings.

Cheddar Cheese Soufflé

"A soufflé you can prepare ahead!"

Serves 6

6 tablespoons butter or margarine
6 tablespoons flour
1 teaspoon salt
½ teaspoon paprika
dash of cayenne
1½ cups milk
6 ounces sharp natural cheddar cheese
(not processed), diced finely (1½ cups)
6 eggs, separated

In double boiler, melt butter, stir in flour, salt, paprika, and cayenne./Add milk all at once, stirring until smooth and thickened./Add cheese and stir until melted./Remove from water./Beat egg yolks and stir into cheese mixture./Beat whites stiff; fold into cheese mixture./Bake uncovered at 350° for 45 minutes or until puffed and golden (do not open oven door until time is up)./Serve at once plain or with a sauce of mushrooms or seafood, or with creamed peas or other vegetable./ Soufflé can be prepared, put in soufflé dish, and refrigerated for as long as 18 hours before baking./To bake, put soufflé in cold oven, set control at 350° and bake 50 minutes./Soufflé can also be frozen a week to 10 days before baking./Bake as for refrigerated soufflé, increasing time to 1½ hours. (Refrigerated or frozen soufflés are slightly more moist.)

Mrs. Robert W. Meserve,
Ladies' Committee Associate

Spinach Frittata

"This recipe is popular in all Italy and especially in the Roman area."

Serves 4

1 pound fresh young spinach
5 large fresh eggs
1 tablespoon crisp precooked bacon
salt and pepper
2 tablespoons fine olive oil

Cook spinach in small amount of water until it is just tender, drain very well, and chop fine./ Beat eggs until they are light and add bacon and salt and pepper./In 8-inch skillet spread olive oil well on bottom over low heat and then add the entire *frittata* mixture./When the mixture is slightly set, transfer to 350° oven and cook until well set./Turn the broiler on to enhance golden brown finish.
This may be served cold or hot and may be made early in the day and reheated./Serve with wedges of Swiss cheese and accompany with tossed salad of fresh young greens.

Mrs. Augustine Bombaci,
Ladies' Committee Associate

No-Crust Cheese and Spinach Pie

"This is a good luncheon dish served with a salad and bread, or it can be an accompaniment for dinner with meat or fish."

Serves 6

1 pound ricotta cheese
1 (10-ounce) package frozen
chopped spinach
1 cup cheese (mozzarella, feta, or cheddar —
or combination), grated
3 eggs, slightly beaten
2 tablespoons oil
½ teaspoon onion salt
½ teaspoon garlic salt
½ teaspoon ground pepper
1-1½ zucchini, sliced and sautéed (optional)
1 cup mushrooms, sliced and sautéed
(optional)
½ cup green pepper, diced and sautéed
(optional)
2 tablespoons butter

Cook spinach and drain./Combine with cheese, eggs, oil, seasonings, and vegetables (if used)./Pour into deep pie plate, lightly oiled./ Dot with butter./Bake at 350° for 40 minutes.

Mrs. Edmund L. Frost,
Ladies' Committee Associate

JOHN WILLIAM HILL (American, 1812–1879)
Study of Fruit. Watercolor
M. and M. Karolik Collection

Stuffed Zucchini Pigeon Cove

"When you haven't looked in your garden recently and suddenly find a great big zucchini, make this all-in-one meal."

Serves 8

1 large zucchini
1 medium onion, chopped
2 tablespoons vegetable oil
½-1 can corned-beef hash
2 tablespoons Parmesan cheese, grated
salt and pepper
1 cup fine bread crumbs
1 egg
1 cup cottage cheese

Slice zucchini lengthwise and scrape out, leaving one third in shell./Chop zucchini and sauté with onion in vegetable oil./Cool./Mix corned-beef hash, Parmesan cheese, salt and pepper, and bread crumbs./Add to zucchini and onion./Mix thoroughly and stuff shells./Beat egg slightly and add cottage cheese./Spread evenly over stuffed shells./Bake at 375° for 60-80 minutes in greased pan./Slice in serving-size pieces.

Elizabeth P. Riegel,
General Manager, Museum Shop

Salmon Loaf

"Left-over loaf is good served cold with herb mayonnaise."

Serves 6

1 (15½-ounce) can Alaska Sockeye
  red salmon
2 cups soft bread crumbs
3 eggs, slightly beaten
½ cup celery, finely chopped
¾ teaspoon salt
¼ teaspoon white pepper
½ teaspoon dill weed

2 tablespoons chives or scallion
  greens, chopped
1 tablespoon lemon juice
¾ teaspoon Worcestershire sauce
½ cup milk
1 bay leaf
1 tablespoon butter

Drain salmon; reserve liquid for sauce./Remove skin from salmon and crush bones (bones are soft, and a good source of calcium)./Mix salmon with crumbs, eggs, celery, salt, pepper, dill weed, chives, lemon juice, and Worcestershire sauce./Mix thoroughly but gently./Add bay leaf to milk in small saucepan; scald./Remove from heat and add butter./When milk is lukewarm, remove bay leaf and pour liquid over salmon mixture./Mix well./Pack into well-buttered 8½ x 4½ x 2½-inch loaf pan; bake at 350° 40-45 minutes, until firm./Let cool about 10 minutes at room temperature before removing from pan./Slice and serve with sauce.

Sauce
3 tablespoons butter
3 tablespoons flour
1 cup liquid (the liquid from salmon can
  plus enough milk to total 1 cup)
½ cup cheddar cheese, grated
salt and pepper
lemon juice or dry white wine (about
  1 tablespoon)
snips of parsley

Melt butter in a small saucepan over medium heat./Stir in flour and cook for about a minute./Add liquid and bring to a boil, stirring continually./Stir in cheese, salt and pepper, lemon juice or wine, and parsley.

Mrs. Richard P. C. Fitzgerald,
Ladies' Committee

• Having a crowd for breakfast? Cook the bacon in the oven. Separate slices and put on a rack in a shallow pan. Bake at 400° for 10 minutes. No turning, no draining.

Puffy Chili Relleno Casserole

"No Mexican would recognize this Americanized dish but it is delicious!"

Serves 6-10

2 (7-ounce) cans whole green chilies
5 corn tortillas cut in wide strips
1 pound Monterey Jack cheese, shredded
1½ large tomatoes, peeled and sliced
8 eggs
½ cup milk
½ teaspoon salt
½ teaspoon pepper
½ teaspoon cumin
½ teaspoon garlic powder
½ teaspoon onion salt
½ teaspoon paprika

Remove seeds from chilies./Lay half the chilies on bottom of a well-greased 9-inch square pan./Top with half the tortilla strips and half the cheese./Arrange all tomato slices on top./Repeat layers of chilies and tortillas and cheese./Beat together eggs, milk, and condiments./Pour evenly over top./Sprinkle lightly with paprika. (Cover and chill if made ahead of time.)/Bake uncovered at 350° about 40 minutes (1 hour if dish is cold) or until puffy and set in center./Let stand about 10 minutes before cutting into squares for serving.

Carol Howard, Gallery Instructor

Delmarva Crab Casserole

"We are a crabmeat-loving family. This is delicious served in scallop shells with rice or on toast points."

Serves 4

1 pound crabmeat
2 cups milk
2 tablespoons flour
¼ teaspoon Dijon mustard
2 tablespoons butter
½ teaspoon salt
dash of cayenne pepper
2 egg yolks
2 tablespoons sherry

Melt butter, add flour and seasonings, and stir in 1½ cups milk./Bring to a boil and cook for 5 minutes./Beat egg yolks until light; add ½ cup milk./Add this mixture to the sauce and cook for 5 minutes./Add sherry and fold in crabmeat.

Mrs. Albert M. Creighton, Jr.
Ladies' Committee Associate

Spinach and Cheese Casserole

"Delicious and different. Can be assembled early in the day and baked just before serving."

Serves 6-8

1 (10-ounce) package frozen chopped spinach
1 (6-ounce) jar marinated artichoke hearts
1 tablespoon margarine or butter
1 medium onion, chopped
¼ teaspoon nutmeg
¾ teaspoon oregano
1 (10½-ounce) can cream of celery soup
4 eggs, beaten
1 (8-ounce) package cream cheese
⅓ cup milk
⅓ cup Parmesan cheese

Squeeze moisture from spinach./Drain artichokes, saving 2 tablespoons marinade./Heat marinade, add margarine in skillet./Cook onion in this until tender./Combine all ingredients except cheeses and milk./Spread in shallow 2-quart buttered baking dish; smooth top./Beat cream cheese, milk, and Parmesan./Spread evenly over spinach./Bake at 350° for 35 minutes or until firm.

Mrs. George N. Proctor,
Ladies' Committee Associate

LEVI WELLS PRENTICE (American, 1850–1935)
Apples in a Tin Pail. Oil painting
Hayden Collection; Charles Henry Hayden Fund

Coucou Sabzi

"Middle Eastern flavor for a delicious omelette."

Serves 6

1½ cups parsley, finely chopped
  (preferably flat-leaf)
¼ cup scallions, finely chopped
¼ cup leeks, finely chopped
½ cup romaine lettuce, finely chopped
¼ cup fresh dill, finely cut
¼ cup fresh mint, finely cut
1 teaspoon oregano
¼ teaspoon turmeric
1 teaspoon salt
½ teaspoon black pepper
½ teaspoon baking powder
3 tablespoons dried currants (optional)
8 eggs
⅓ cup olive oil

Combine the ingredients in a deep bowl./Add the eggs and 2 tablespoons of the olive oil./ Beat vigorously with a fork./In a 10-inch covered skillet, heat the remaining oil until a light haze forms./Pour in the herb and egg mixture, spreading it out evenly with a spatula./Cover and cook over low heat for 8-10 minutes./Run a knife around the pan to free the *coucou* and lift with a flat utensil./Cover the skillet with a flat plate, invert (watch out for the hot oil), and turn the *coucou* out on the plate./Then carefully slide it back into the skillet./Cover again and cook for 4-5 more minutes./Serve hot or cold with yogurt or sour cream.

Edward Brovarski,
Assistant Curator,
Egyptian and Ancient Near Eastern Art

Spaghetti Pie

"I usually prepare two of these pies at the same time and freeze one. Good with green salad and French bread for a quick supper."

Serves 6

6 ounces spaghetti (8 ounces linguini)
2 tablespoons butter
½ cup Parmesan cheese, freshly grated
2 eggs, well beaten
1 pound ground beef or pork sausage
½ cup onion, chopped
¼ cup green pepper, chopped
1 (8-ounce) can tomatoes, cut up
1 (6-ounce) can tomato paste
1 teaspoon sugar
1 teaspoon dried oregano, crushed
½ teaspoon garlic salt
1 cup cottage cheese
½ cup mozzarella cheese, shredded

Butter a 10-inch pie plate./Cook spaghetti and drain (makes 3¼ cups of spaghetti)./Stir butter into hot spaghetti./Stir in Parmesan cheese and eggs./Form spaghetti mixture into a crust in 10-inch pie plate./In skillet cook ground beef or pork sausage, onion, and green pepper until vegetables are tender and meat is browned./ Drain off fat./Stir in undrained tomatoes, tomato paste, sugar, oregano, and garlic salt./ Spread cottage cheese over bottom of spaghetti crust./Fill pie with tomato-meat mixture./ Bake at 350° for 30 minutes./Sprinkle with mozzarella cheese./Bake 5 minutes longer. Freezes well./If you plan to freeze pie, do not add mozzarella until final baking.

Katherine B. Duane,
Operations Coordinator

▪ **A special butter for a special breakfast: honey and Amaretto or Grand Marnier beaten into unsalted butter.**

Tomato Pie Niçoise

"Absolutely delicious!"

Serves 6-8

1 two-crust prepared pastry
½ cup soft bread crumbs, buttered
1 cup small peas, canned or frozen
4 small firm tomatoes, either green or ripe, thinly sliced
2 tablespoons melted butter or olive oil
1 can flat anchovy fillets, drained
1 large clove of garlic, minced
1 large white onion, thinly sliced and separated into rings
pepper, freshly ground
½ cup stuffed olives, sliced
2 tablespoons tomato paste, thinned with 3 tablespoons sherry

Line a pie plate with pastry./Cover with buttered crumbs./Layer on peas and half of the tomato slices, drizzling with 1 tablespoon butter or olive oil./Top with anchovy fillets and minced garlic./Cover with layer of onion rings, then remaining tomato slices./Drizzle on 1 tablespoon butter or oil and sprinkle with pepper to taste./Top with sliced olives./Cover with top crust and seal./Cut several slashes in the crust to allow steam to escape./Bake at 450° for 10 minutes, reduce temperature to 375° and continue baking about 20 minutes more or until browned./Just before serving, pour into pie through slashes the tomato paste thinned with sherry.

Mrs. Francis R. Kenney,
Ladies' Committee Associate

Mushroom Pancake Tower

"A delicious luncheon or supper dish, served with a green salad. Instead of mushrooms, crabmeat or lobster make a delicious filling."

Serves 4-6

Batter
¾ stick butter or margarine
2 tablespoons flour
¼ cup milk
3 egg yolks
salt and pepper
3 egg whites, beaten stiff

Make a light roux by melting butter in saucepan, adding flour and cooking over low heat for 2 minutes, stirring constantly./Cool, add egg yolks, salt and pepper, and fold in beaten egg whites./From this batter make 4 pancakes about 5 inches in diameter, cooking over medium heat just until golden.

Filling
½ pound fresh mushrooms, sliced
1 tablespoon onion, minced
1 teaspoon parsley, minced
2 tablespoons butter
salt and pepper
paprika

Sauté mushrooms, onion, and parsley in butter and season with salt, pepper, and paprika.

Topping
2 or 3 tablespoons sour cream
Parmesan cheese, grated

Butter a casserole and place one pancake on the bottom./Spread with one third of filling; place another pancake on top, then another third of filling, the third pancake, and remaining filling with last layer a pancake./Spread the top with sour cream and sprinkle with a little or a lot of Parmesan cheese, depending on your liking./Bake, uncovered, in a 375° oven for 30 minutes./Serve hot.

Suzanne Chapman,
Associate Curator Emeritus,
Egyptian and Ancient Near Eastern Art

WINSLOW HOMER (American, 1836–1910)
Going Berrying, 1879. Crayon drawing
Bequest of the estate of Katharine Dexter McCormick

Curried Crab with Almonds

"Crunchy toasted almonds give texture and flavor to this delicious curry dish."

Serves 6

2 tablespoons butter
2 tablespoons flour
1 cup milk or cream, scalded slowly
salt and pepper
3 cups flaked crabmeat
⅓ cup butter
1½ tablespoons onion, grated
2 tablespoons curry powder
⅓ cup slivered almonds, toasted

Melt butter and gradually add flour./Cook the roux, stirring constantly, over low heat for 3-5 minutes./Add 1 cup scalded milk or cream, stirring constantly to blend well./Season with salt and pepper./Cook over hot but not boiling water until thick and smooth.

In a skillet sauté crabmeat in butter until the crab is hot and well coated with butter. Season hot white sauce with onion and curry powder and cook sauce, stirring until the ingredients are blended./Add the sauce to the crabmeat, mix well, and stir in slivered almonds.

Serve over fluffy rice.

Suzanne Chapman,
Associate Curator Emeritus,
Egyptian and Ancient Near Eastern Art

Cannelloni alla Toscana

"This was a lunch specialty at a small terrace tearoom on the west coast many years ago."

Serves 6

Filling
3 cups cooked chicken, finely chopped
¾ cup ricotta or cottage cheese
½ cup spinach, well drained and chopped
½ teaspoon nutmeg
salt, pepper, and paprika to taste

Mix and form into cigar-size shapes.

Crepes
3 eggs
¼ teaspoon salt
1½ cups milk
1 cup flour

Beat these ingredients in a blender, then let set 2 hours (makes 12 crepes)./Place filling in the crepes.

Topping
3 tablespoons butter
2 tablespoons flour
1⅓ cups cream
½ teaspoon salt
¼ teaspoon pepper
Tomato sauce
Parmesan cheese

Cook flour in butter over low heat for 2 minutes./Add cream, salt, and pepper./In a shallow casserole place approximately 2 cups Italian-type tomato sauce ¼ inch deep./Add filled crepes and pour over all 1½ cups white sauce./Top with ⅓ cup Parmesan cheese./Bake at 350° for ½ hour.

Mrs. Frank Clapp,
Ladies' Committee Associate

Plantation Vegetable Pie

"Unusual and delicious."

Serves 6

1 (9-inch) prepared pie shell
1 cup Parmesan cheese, freshly grated
1 medium eggplant, peeled and sliced
¼ cup vegetable oil
2 medium onions, peeled and sliced
2 large tomatoes, sliced

Sprinkle half of Parmesan cheese into unbaked pie crust./Sauté eggplant slices in oil until tender./Drain on paper towels./Sauté sliced onions./Layer eggplant, sliced tomatoes, onions, and cheese in pie crust, ending with cheese./Bake 40-45 minutes at 350°./Cut into wedges.

Mrs. Clarence A. Kemper,
Ladies' Committee

Mushroom Casserole

"Instead of stuffing mushrooms, the same flavor, with less work or watching, may be achieved with the following recipe."

Serves 8

1 pound mushrooms
1 cup plain bread crumbs
2 tablespoons parsley, minced
3 tablespoons Parmesan cheese
¼ teaspoon pepper
½ teaspoon salt
2 tablespoons olive oil
¼ teaspoon oregano

Wash mushrooms, dry and chop, using stems as well./Mix together with all ingredients./ Put into buttered casserole and bake at 350° for about 20 minutes./For cocktails, leave mushrooms whole, and let guests use cocktail picks to serve themselves.

Mrs. Frederick P. Costanza,
Ladies' Committee Associate

Mexican Shrimp

"South of the border flavor."

Serves 4-6

2 tablespoons butter
1 small onion, chopped
½ cup celery, chopped
6 ounces green chili sauce
1 tablespoon steak sauce
½ tablespoon salt
1 cup sour cream
1 pound cooked shrimp

Melt butter; cook onion and celery until soft./ Blend in chili sauce, steak sauce and salt./Add sour cream and heat./Do not allow to boil./ Add shrimp; heat and serve./Delicious served over fluffy rice, with cooked artichoke hearts.

Mrs. James H. Cannon,
Ladies' Committee Associate

Spinach-Tomato Quiche

"A delicious variation of quiche given me by an English friend."

Serves 8

pastry for 11-inch quiche
1 package frozen chopped spinach
1 clove garlic, crushed
1 tablespoon butter
3 or 4 tomatoes, sliced and seeded
½ pound mushrooms, sautéed in butter
   and seasoned
6-8 ounces sharp cheddar cheese, grated
4 eggs
1 tablespoon cornstarch
¾ cup milk
¾ cup cream
½ teaspoon salt
¼ teaspoon pepper

Prepare pastry for one 11-inch quiche pan or 2 smaller ones./Cook spinach, drain and reheat with garlic and butter./In pastry shell, spread spinach evenly on bottom./Sprinkle with some of the grated cheese./Add the tomatoes, more cheese, mushrooms, and more cheese, saving about 2 tablespoons for the top./Beat eggs, cornstarch, milk and cream, salt, and pepper./Pour over filling, sprinkle top with remaining cheese./Bake 45-60 minutes at 375°./Cool 10 minutes before cutting.

Mrs. Charles Winans,
Ladies' Committee Associate

Louisiana Shrimp Creole

"A cherished old family recipe from the bayous of Louisiana."

Serves 8

¼ cup flour
¼ cup vegetable oil
2 cups onions, chopped
1 clove garlic, minced
1 cup green pepper, chopped
2 (15-ounce) cans tomato sauce
3 pounds peeled, raw shrimp
1 cup water
1 teaspoon salt
¼ teaspoon black pepper
½ teaspoon Tabasco
2 teaspoons Worcestershire sauce
1½ cups celery, finely chopped
½ cup parsley, chopped
¼ cup green onion tops, chopped
2 bay leaves
2 thin lemon slices

In heavy pot make a roux by stirring the oil and flour together over medium high heat until it turns a caramel color./Add onions, garlic, and green pepper and sauté until onions are transparent and soft./Add tomato sauce, stir, and simmer 5 minutes./Add peeled, raw shrimp (frozen shrimp which have been rinsed in a colander may be used.)/Gradually add about 1 cup water to thin./Simmer to blend./Do not boil./Add remaining ingredients./Cover and simmer gently for 30 minutes, stirring occasionally./Remove bay leaves and lemon slices./Serve over hot, fluffy rice. (May be made a day ahead./If so, heat without boiling and serve immediately./Freezes well.)

Mrs. Clarence A. Kemper, Ladies' Committee

▪ **"Tell me what you eat, and I will tell you what you are."**

Brillat-Savarin

Antipasto Loaf

"Nice for a summer lunch or buffet."

Serves 6-8

Bean filling
1 (1-pound) can white kidney beans, drained and rinsed
2 tablespoons vinegar
2 tablespoons salad oil
½ cup parsley, finely chopped
¼ cup scallions, chopped
1 (4-ounce) jar pimientos, drained and chopped
1 tablespoon capers
salt and pepper

Mix all ingredients and pack into foil-lined 4-cup loaf pan or round bowl.

Tuna filling
2 (7-ounce) cans tuna in oil, drained
4 hard-cooked eggs, chopped
1 cup ripe olives, pitted and sliced
⅓ cup mayonnaise
¼ cup celery, finely chopped
1 tablespoon onion, grated
1 tablespoon lemon juice
salt

Combine and press on top of bean mixture./ Cover with foil and chill./Unmold onto a platter./Since there is no gelatin in this, don't expect it to keep perfect shape.

Eve Skinner, Gallery Instructor

Baked Cottage Cheese

"This recipe reaches back to my grandmother's grandmother. A boon for vegetarians. Serve as a luncheon dish with a tart salad and full-bodied red wine."

Yield: about 30 cakes

1 (32-ounce) carton cottage cheese
1 (7½-ounce) package farmer's cheese
1 egg
2 cups flour
salt and black pepper, freshly ground

Mix ingredients together to the consistency of a rich dough./Fashion uniform flat cakes of the mixture and roll each one lightly in flour./Drop them into a large kettle of boiling salted water./Do not cover the kettle./Cook a few at a time./They will rise from bottom of pan./Remove with slotted spoon and arrange in a generously buttered baking pan or pie plate.*/Drizzle melted butter between the patties and over them./Bake at 375° for about 20-25 minutes, until all bubbly and buttery./Add a generous amount of fresh ground pepper./Salt as your conscience allows.

Doris Powell,
Secretary to Ladies' Committee

*Save the liquid for Country Soup recipe on page 53

Macaroni with Four Cheeses

"Better than the usual macaroni and cheese."

Serves 6-8

1 pound macaroni
1 cup Fontina, diced
1 cup Bel Paese, diced
1 cup Gruyère, diced
1 cup Parmesan, grated
¼ cup tomato sauce
¼ cup cream
¼ teaspoon dried rosemary
¼ teaspoon dried oregano
¼ teaspoon dried basil
5 slices of bacon, diced

Cook macaroni according to package directions./Melt cheeses in tomato sauce and cream./Add rosemary, oregano, and basil./Cook bacon until golden, but not too crisp./Drain./Toss cooked macaroni in cheese sauce, then garnish with bacon.

Mrs. Selwyn A. Kudisch,
Ladies' Committee Associate

Fines Herbes Pâté

"A favorite at Museum functions."

Serves 8-10

1 pound ground pork
5 ounces fresh spinach, chopped and blanched (or frozen package)
4 ounces chicken liver, blanched in boiling water, cooled and diced
4 ounces ham, diced
3 tablespoons parsley, chopped
1 tablespoon fresh basil, chopped (or 1 teaspoon dry)
½ cup onion, finely chopped
1 large clove fresh garlic, crushed
1 pinch (between thumb, index, and middle fingers) rosemary
1 pinch nutmeg
1 pinch black pepper
1 pinch white pepper
1 pinch poultry seasoning
1 teaspoon salt, or more
2 teaspoons plain gelatin
½ cup light cream
bacon strips

Combine all ingredients and mix thoroughly./Line a pâté pan (or bread pan) with strips of bacon./Cook at 350° for 1½ hours, in a pan filled with water to prevent burning of the bottom./After taking out of the oven, use a weight the same size as the pan (a clean brick) to put pressure on pâté while cooling in the refrigerator overnight./Unmold, slice, and enjoy.

Chef Alfred Georgs,
Museum Restaurant

Moo Goo Gai Pan

"One of my favorites. Prepare ingredients ahead, cook at the last minute."

Serves 4-6

1½ pounds boneless spring chicken breasts
salt and pepper
1 tablespoon sherry
1 tablespoon cornstarch
½ egg white
4 tablespoons oil
1 teaspoon salt
12 mushrooms, sliced
2 stalks celery, sliced
1 can water chestnuts, sliced
1 package frozen snow peas
1 clove garlic, sliced
2-3 stalks scallions
2 tablespoons soy sauce
½ tablespoon sugar

Slice or cube chicken meat and mix with salt, pepper, sherry, cornstarch, and egg white./ Heat 2 tablespoons oil and add salt./Sauté mushrooms, celery, water chestnuts, and snow peas for 2 minutes./Remove from pan./Heat 2 tablespoons oil in same pan./Fry garlic, scallions, and chicken for 1 minute over high heat./Add soy sauce and sugar and mix well./ Add cooked vegetables and mix well for 1 minute./Remove to heated plate./Serve with rice and mandarin oranges.

Jane H. Bryant, Gallery Instructor

Coronation Chicken

"This recipe was served at the luncheon for Queen Elizabeth, following her coronation."

Serves 6-8

2 young roasting chickens (or equivalent
  chicken breasts)

Poach the chickens with carrot, bouquet garni, salt, and 4 peppercorns in water and a little wine (enough to barely cover) for 40 minutes or until tender./Cool chicken in its own juices, remove bones, keep meat in large pieces./ Prepare the sauce given below.

Cream of Curry Sauce
1 tablespoon oil
3 tablespoons onion, finely chopped
1 teaspoon curry powder
1 teaspoon tomato purée
½ cup red wine
⅓ cup water
1 bay leaf
salt, sugar, and pepper
1-2 slices lemon and squeeze of lemon
1½ cups mayonnaise
1-2 tablespoons apricot purée
2-3 tablespoons cream, lightly whipped
a little extra whipped cream

Heat the oil, add onion, cook gently 3-4 minutes, add curry powder./Cook again 1-2 minutes./Add tomato purée, wine, water, and bay leaf./Bring to boil, add salt, sugar to taste, pepper, lemon, and lemon juice./Simmer uncovered for 5-10 minutes./Strain and cool./ Add by degrees to the mayonnaise with the apricot purée to taste./Adjust seasoning, adding a little more lemon if necessary./Finish with the whipped cream./Reserve a small amount of sauce (enough to coat the chicken) and mix with a little extra cream and seasoning./Mix rest of sauce with chicken./ Arrange in serving dish and coat with extra sauce (also a delicious sauce to serve with cold lobster).

Rice Salad
The rice salad that accompanied the chicken was of cooked rice, cooked peas, diced raw cucumber, and finely chopped mixed herbs, all mixed in a well-seasoned French dressing./Or use the rice salad on page 84.

Mrs. Charles Winans,
Ladies' Committee Associate

ANONYMOUS CHINESE (Yuan Dynasty; 14th century)
Vendor of Sweetmeats and Child. Hanging scroll. Ink and color
Charles B. Hoyt Collection

Old Appian Way Asparagus Frittata

"This method of making frittata is as old as the ancient Appian Way itself. Served with a fresh tossed green salad and crusty Italian bread, it makes a luncheon dish both satisfying and pretty."

Serves 4

1 pound fresh young asparagus, cooked and cut into ½-inch pieces
6 large eggs
1 tablespoon fresh parsley, chopped
¼ cup Parmesan cheese, freshly grated
salt and pepper
1 tablespoon olive oil

Cook asparagus and set aside to drain, squeezing out all moisture./Beat eggs until light./Add parsley and Parmesan cheese, mixing well./Add asparagus, being sure it is drained well./Salt and pepper./Spread about 1 tablespoon olive oil in bottom of 9-inch cast-iron skillet./Heat about 1 minute and add complete mixture and cook over low heat until it sets, being careful it doesn't stick./When lightly browned on bottom, transfer the skillet to 350° oven and let set completely or until dry in center./Turn broiler on for 1 minute to color golden.

This may be served hot or cold and can be made early in the day and reheated if desired.

Mrs. Augustine Bombaci,
Ladies' Committee Associate

Denver Sandwich Ring

"A delicious luncheon dish. I pour the sauce into a small bowl and place it in the center of the sandwich ring."

Serves 4-6

1½ cups buttermilk pancake/waffle mix
⅓ cup cooking oil
¼ cup milk
1 egg

1½ cups cooked ham, finely cubed
⅓ cup onion, finely chopped
⅓ cup green pepper, chopped

Combine pancake mix, oil, milk, and eggs./Stir until blended./Stir in ham, onion, and green pepper; mix well./Drop by heaping tablespoons in a ring around edge of ungreased pizza pan or other 12-inch oven-proof dish./Bake at 425° for 15-20 minutes or until golden brown.

Sauce
1 can condensed cheddar cheese soup
⅓ cup milk

Add milk to soup and heat slowly, stirring often./Serve sauce over wedges of sandwich ring.

Mrs. Joseph A. Valatka,
Ladies' Committee Associate

Crevettes et Avocats Vinaigrettes

"The most delicious salad I've ever eaten! Served at one of our first gourmet dinners."

Serves 6

1 pound cooked shrimp
3 avocados
¼ teaspoon dry mustard
½ teaspoon salt
¼ teaspoon black pepper
⅓ cup olive oil
3 tablespoons wine vinegar
1 onion, chopped
1 clove garlic, minced

Shell shrimp and cut into small pieces./Cut the avocados in half and carefully scrape out meat, reserving shells./Cube the avocado meat and combine with shrimp.

Mix mustard, salt, and pepper in a bowl./Gradually add the oil, mixing carefully until the spices are dissolved./Add the vinegar, onion, and garlic and beat well./Pour over shrimp and avocado mixture and mix carefully./Fill shells with mixture.

Jane H. Bryant, Gallery Instructor

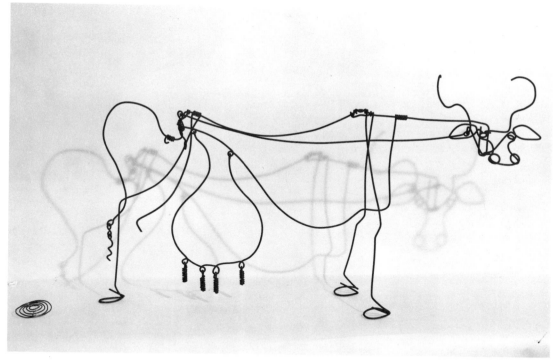

ALEXANDER CALDER (American, 1898–1976)
Cow, ca. 1926. Brass wire
Decorative Arts Special Fund

Red-Flannel Hash

"No cruise is complete without this one."

Serves 4-6

¼ pound bacon (4-5 slices), chopped
1 medium onion, diced
6 medium beets, precooked and diced
6 medium potatoes, precooked and diced
1 cup cooked corned beef, chopped
2 tablespoons cream
1 tablespoon parsley

Fry bacon until it begins to brown./Add onions./When onions become translucent, stir in beets, potatoes, and corned beef./Spread the mixture evenly throughout the pan./Cook uncovered over low heat until bottom browns (about 40 minutes)./Add cream and parsley./Fold and serve.

Maurice ("Peter") Tonissi II, Esq.,
Receptionist, Members' Room

Cowboy Beans

"Great picnic fare."

Serves 4

12 slices bacon
1 medium onion
1 (1-pound, 12-ounce) can beans with pork
and tomato sauce
½ cup dark brown sugar
1 cup red wine

Fry bacon until crisp./Drain./Slice onion into thin rings and sauté in the bacon fat until golden./In a large casserole empty the beans./Add sugar and wine./Crumble the bacon and add with the onion to the casserole./Bake at 350° for 1½ hours, covered./Add more wine if it reduces too much. (This is best made the day before and reheated.)

Mrs. Fred Glimp,
Ladies' Committee Associate

JEROME B. THOMPSON (American, 1814–1886)
"Pic Nick," Camden, Maine. Oil painting
M. and M. Karolik Collection

The Best of Soups

Ale or Beer and Cheddar Soup

"Beer adds a distinctive tang to this soup."

Yield: 4½ quarts

12 ounces butter or margarine (1½ sticks)
⅔ cup celery, finely chopped
⅔ cup carrots, finely chopped
⅔ cup onion, finely chopped
¾ cup flour
1½ tablespoons dry mustard
3 quarts chicken broth, or good meat stock
1 pound sharp cheddar, grated
Tabasco
1 quart beer or ale

Melt margarine or butter and sauté the vegetables until soft./Add flour to pick up the fat and add dry mustard./Add 3 quarts chicken broth (or good meat stock) and cheddar./Season with Tabasco to taste./Last, add 1 quart or more of beer or ale.

Chef Alfred Georgs,
Museum Restaurant

Blizzard Soup

"First made during blizzard of '78; make it when you have pork shoulder and put away for the next snowstorm. Freezes well."

Yield: about 2 quarts

2 celery stalks, chopped
1 carrot, chopped
1 onion, chopped
3 tablespoons butter or oil
3 tablespoons flour
6 cups stock from pork shoulder with meat
1 bay leaf
¼ teaspoon thyme
1½ cups lentils, washed
salt

Make stock from pork shoulder./Leave plenty of meat on the bone and include the meat bits in the stock./Heat butter or oil in large saucepan and stir in vegetables./Cover, cook over low heat, stirring occasionally, until vegetables are tender, about 10 minutes./Blend in the flour./Cook 2 minutes, stirring./Remove pan from heat./Gradually blend in 1 cup hot stock, stirring to blend thoroughly./Pour in the rest of the liquid and bring to a simmer./Add herbs and stir in the lentils and salt./Cover pan loosely and simmer slowly 1¼-1½ hours, until lentils are very tender./Purée the soup in a food mill or blender and return to heat./Add more liquid if it is too thick./Good with garlic croutons.

Mrs. Marsden P. Earle,
Ladies' Committee

Fish Soup

"Quick, easy soup—especially with food processor!"

Serves 4

2 tablespoons oil
2 onions, chopped
3 cloves of garlic, chopped
2 teaspoons paprika
2 teaspoons curry powder
4 medium ripe tomatoes, chopped and seeded
4 cups chicken or fish stock
1 pound fish fillet, cut into bite-size pieces
1 teaspoon salt
pepper, freshly ground

Sauté onions and garlic in oil over low heat for about 10 minutes./Add paprika, curry powder, tomatoes, and stock./Bring to a boil./Reduce heat to simmer./Add fish, salt, and pepper, and cook for about 6 minutes or until fish is white and opaque.

Mrs. Earle W. Wilkins,
Ladies' Committee Associate

Consommé Mousse

"This easy made-ahead recipe is my favorite for a first course. It can wait indefinitely for that person who has just been given a cocktail. I first had it in Ireland."

Serves 4

1 (13-ounce) can consommé
2 (3-ounce) packages cream cheese
1 teaspoon curry (optional)

Put aside ¼ cup of consommé, put all other ingredients in blender, and blend until smooth./Pour into individual dishes; put in refrigerator for 2 hours./When set, pour on top the reserve consommé./When that is set, garnish with chopped chives.

Mrs. Morgan K. Smith,
Ladies' Committee Associate

Eggplant Stew

"A delicious Greek recipe from my husband's great-grandmother, who brought it from Tenos."

Serves 4-6

1 pound ground beef, browned and
    crumbled
2 tablespoons onion, chopped
1 medium eggplant, peeled and diced in
    ¼-inch cubes
1 large can tomatoes, whole
large bunch fresh thyme, chopped
    (or ½ teaspoon dried)
2 tablespoons parsley, chopped
salt and pepper

Combine all ingredients./Simmer 30-45 minutes or until nicely blended and vegetables are tender (or bake at 350° for 30-45 minutes)./Serve with rice, or by itself with salad of tomatoes, feta cheese, green olives, and green pepper.

Mrs. Victor A. Lutnicki, Ladies' Committee

• Serve jellied madrilene in avocado halves. Top with a dollop of sour cream and caviar.

Oven Fish Chowder

"A delicious fish chowder, quite different. Easy."

Serves 6

2 pounds cod fillets
1 package scalloped potatoes
    (including seasonings)
2 bay leaves
2 whole cloves
3 onions, sliced
¼ cup butter or margarine
¼ teaspoon pepper
½ teaspoon thyme
4 cups boiling water
2 cups light cream
½ cup white wine
parsley, chopped

Put all ingredients except last 3 in a large casserole./Add 4 cups boiling water./Mix together./Cover and bake at 375° for 1½ hours./Heat cream to scalding point./Add to chowder./Remove bay leaves and cloves./Add wine and garnish with parsley. (If there is not enough liquid add milk.)/This also adapts to a slow cooker.

Mrs. Allan R. Finlay,
Ladies' Committee Associate

Spinach Soup

"Pale green and delicious, hot or cold."

Serves 8

2 packages frozen spinach, thawed
1 onion, minced
4 tablespoons butter
4 tablespoons flour
4 cups chicken broth
1 or more cups light cream
¼ cup vermouth
nutmeg
salt and pepper

Sauté onions in butter until translucent./Add flour and cook, stirring a few minutes. Remove from heat./Add hot broth, return to heat, bring to a boil, and cook until smooth. Add spinach./ Purée in blender or food processor until smooth./Add cream, vermouth, and seasonings to taste./Excellent cold, too.

Mrs. Richard Wengren,
Ladies' Committee

Super Stew

"Good make-ahead dish. Improves on the second day."

Serves 8

3 pounds stew meat
3 onions, chopped
3 tablespoons margarine
3 carrots, sliced
3 potatoes, peeled and cut in chunks
1 can tomato paste
½ cup water with 1 teaspoon beef stock base
   added
½ teaspoon dry mustard
¼ cup brown sugar
salt and pepper
½ cup chutney
½ cup catsup

Brown meat and onions in margarine./Add carrots and potatoes, then tomato paste, water, beef stock base, mustard, brown sugar, and salt and pepper./Cover and simmer 1 hour./Add chutney and catsup./Bake covered at 250° for 1¾ hours.

Mrs. R. Willis Leith, Jr.
Ladies' Committee

• **To make quick onion soup, gently sauté sweet onions in butter until golden. Add canned consommé and simmer. Place in oven-proof bowls, top with toasted rounds of French bread sprinkled liberally with grated Gruyère cheese. Bake in a hot oven until cheese browns.**

Stefado

"A Greek onion stew with beef."

Serves 4-6

2-3 pounds lean beef
3 tablespoons butter
½ (6-ounce) can tomato paste
1 clove garlic, chopped (or powder,
   if preferred)
1 bay leaf
1-2 tablespoons wine vinegar
salt and pepper
water
1-2 pounds small white onions
1 cup walnut halves
feta cheese

Cut beef into 1-inch cubes and brown in butter in pot or casserole./Add tomato paste, garlic, bay leaf, wine vinegar, salt, and pepper and enough water to cover./Bring to a boil, cover, and simmer for 1½-2 hours until meat is tender./Add white onions and simmer for 20 minutes or until onions are cooked./Add walnut halves and continue to simmer for 15 minutes./During the last 5 minutes of cooking add cubes of feta cheese.

Mrs. George D. Mason,
Ladies' Committee Associate

Jane Noel's Summer Soup

"A refreshing, delicious summer soup!"

Serves 6

1 can tomato soup
1 cup chicken broth
1 medium cucumber, peeled
1 small onion
7 or 8 sprigs of parsley
1 cup light cream

Whir everything but the cream in a blender until smooth./Chill (even better if made the day before)./Stir in cream just before serving.

Miss Ellen Stillman,
Ladies' Committee Associate

Yogurt Soup

"When I have served this, no one has been able to guess that the main ingredient is yogurt. Even non-yogurt eaters will relish this."

Serves 8-10

4 cups plain yogurt
4 cups water
1 egg
salt to taste
1½ cups egg noodles, broken
1 medium onion, chopped
1 garlic clove, minced
5 tablespoons butter or margarine
2 tablespoons dried mint

Mix yogurt, water, egg, and salt in a 4-quart saucepan./Cook over a high flame until the mixture comes to a boil./Add the noodles, lower flame, and cook until the noodles are tender (about 10 minutes)./Add the onion and garlic, which have been sautéed in butter along with the mint, and cook an additional 5 minutes./Best made the day before and refrigerated./Heat through to serve (if too thick, more water may be added).

Mrs. Malcolm L. Trayser,
Ladies' Committee Associate

Zucchini Soup

"Pale green and delicious!"

Serves 4

1 large onion, chopped
2 tablespoons butter
2 cups chicken broth
2 cups zucchini, grated (do not peel)
¼ cup parsley leaves
½ teaspoon salt
⅛ teaspoon each: garlic salt, celery salt, and
  nutmeg

Sauté onion in butter until soft./Add chicken broth, grated zucchini, seasonings, and parsley./Cook 10 minutes./Purée in blender or food processor./Add ¾ cup cream and reheat, but do not boil./May be served hot or cold.

Howard W. Johnson, Trustee

Zucchini and Tomato Soup

"Delicious hot or cold. Make a day ahead."

Serves 8

¼ cup parsley leaves
1 tablespoon chives
2 medium onions, peeled and quartered
  (1½ cup minced)
2 large tomatoes, peeled, seeded, and
  quartered (¾ cup, coarsely chopped)
6 small zucchini
1 teaspoon salt
2 tablespoons oil
4 cups chicken stock
½ teaspoon sugar
½ teaspoon oregano
½ teaspoon basil
2 teaspoons lemon juice
salt and pepper
nutmeg, grated

With steel blade of food processor, mince parsley and chives and reserve for garnish./Mince onions and set aside./Chop tomatoes coarsely and set aside./With slicer, slice zucchini; reserve 8 slices for garnish.

In a large pot, heat oil; add onion and zucchini, cover and sauté slowly 10 minutes, add stock and simmer 20 minutes./With steel blade purée zucchini./Return purée to pot, add tomatoes, sugar, oregano, basil, lemon juice, salt and pepper, and nutmeg to taste./Cook 5 minutes; thin with stock or cream if desired./Serve hot or chilled./Garnish with zucchini slices, parsley, and chives.

Mrs. John A. Pooley,
Ladies' Committee

• **Spread Syrian bread with melted butter and sesame seeds. Bake at 400° until golden.**

GUY ARNOUX (French, d. 1951). *Le Parfait Cuisinier François*. Wood engraving from
Les Jeunes Héros de France, ca. 1917 (Paris: Devambez). Bequest of W.G. Russell Allen

Low-Tide Bisque

"As a child growing up in Marblehead I derived most of my fun from the sea – in it, on it, or near it. Although it curtailed the swimming, low tide brought me the greatest pleasure. Then the rocks revealed their secrets – nooks, crannies, and caves known only to their inhabitants became visible and explorable. The beach, which was as much a part of my childhood as my one-room schoolhouse, gradually enlarged itself, exposing an enormous carpet of crystal shimmering in the sun. Then I could pull mussels from the rocks and dig the clams from the sand. However, gathering mussels or clams is a task for the hardy and the experienced, not for the child blessed solely with enthusiasm. I usually returned to the kitchen with 12 mussels and 12 clams. With a family of 4 what can you do with only 24 bivalves? My mother had the answer. She made soup. Here is her recipe with a few variations, which came quite naturally and tastefully over the last fifty years."

Serves 6

12 mussels
12 clams
1 cup dry white wine
generous amount of fresh basil and parsley
½ teaspoon salt
½ teaspoon pepper, freshly ground
2 cloves garlic, minced
1 small onion, sliced
2 tablespoons butter
2 cups cold water
3 tablespoons butter
2 tablespoons flour
1 cup all-purpose cream
2 egg yolks

Scrub mussels and clams and place them in a deep kettle./Add wine, basil, parsley, salt, pepper, garlic, onion, and 2 tablespoons butter./Cover./Bring to boil./Reduce heat and simmer for 2 minutes./Add 2 cups cold water./Simmer gently for 5 minutes or until clams and mussels open./(Discard any that don't.)/Strain the broth and reserve./Remove meat from the shells and place in blender with 2 cups of the reserved broth./Blend at high speed for 2 minutes./Heat 3 tablespoons of butter in a saucepan./Add flour and stir over low heat until well blended./Add gradually the blended broth and stir./Cook gently until bisque begins to thicken./Slowly add all-purpose cream and cook gently until bisque is hot but not boiling./Beat the egg yolks and add a little of the warm soup, stirring while adding the soup. Add this mixture to the soup, stirring constantly until the soup is thickened and hot but not boiling./Correct the seasoning if necessary./Serve in hot soup bowls./Garnish with chopped fresh parsley and a swirl of butter.

Clementine Brown, Manager,
Public Information (with thanks to
Libby Alsberg of Marblehead)

Avocado Velvet

"Just the soup for a warm summer day."

Serves 4-5

1 cup ripe avocado, puréed (about 1 good-
  sized avocado)
1 cup sour cream
1 cup chicken stock (or canned
  chicken broth)
rind of 1 orange, grated
pinch of cayenne
salt and lemon juice
1 hard-cooked egg, minced
watercress

Mix all the ingredients except egg and watercress./Chill and serve in crystal bowls./Garnish with egg and watercress.

Mrs. J. Wallace McMeel,
Ladies' Committee Associate

Cream of Zucchini Soup

"I make quarts of this every summer. The curry flavor is what makes this somewhat standard recipe unusual."

Serves 4

1 pound young zucchini, sliced
2 tablespoons butter
2 tablespoons onion, minced
1 clove garlic, minced
1 teaspoon curry powder
salt and pepper
1¾ cups chicken broth
½ cup light cream

Sauté zucchini with onion and garlic in butter, covered, for 15 minutes or until tender./Add curry powder and salt and pepper./Spoon mixture into blender; add broth and cream./Blend well and serve hot or cold with croutons or chopped chives.

Mrs. John W. White, Trustee

Country Soup

"A nutritious, indefinable country soup."

Yield: 4 quarts

1 large can of tomatoes
1 medium-sized onion, chopped
4 tablespoons flour
4 tablespoons butter
3 cups milk
bay leaf
½ teaspoon baking soda

Add the canned tomatoes to the liquid in the kettle in which cottage cheese cakes (see page 40) were cooked./Add bay leaf; cook for 15 minutes./Sauté the onion in a little butter and add to the pot./Remove from heat and add the baking soda./Make a thin white sauce with the flour, butter, and milk./Add the tomato mixture to the sauce to avoid curdling, then gradually warm the entire mixture./Do not boil.

*Doris Powell,
Secretary to the Ladies' Committee*

Pumpkin Soup

"You can do more with a pumpkin than make it into a pie."

Serves 6

1 (15-ounce) can pumpkin, or equivalent of
    fresh pumpkin, steamed and mashed
¼ cup potato, mashed
1 cup canned tomatoes, seeded
2 cups chicken stock or bouillon
nutmeg and allspice
cream and/or milk
salt and pepper

Cook vegetables in stock until well blended./Purée in a blender if you like a smooth soup, or leave as is for more texture./Season to taste./Thin with milk and/or cream according to the richness you want./Serve hot./A dollop of sour cream sprinkled with a few roasted pumpkin seeds makes a good garnish.

*Mrs. Selwyn A. Kudisch,
Ladies' Committee*

Kalte Schale

"Use red currants, raspberries, strawberries, or blueberries for this traditional German fruit soup."

Serves 18-20

4 cups of berries
1 gallon of water
juice and rind of 1 lemon
1 cinnamon stick
6-8 whole cloves
1 cup sugar (or more, according to taste)
20 ounces fruit-flavored gelatin (use lemon
    with blueberries, raspberry with other
    berries)

Bring everything except the gelatin to a boil and simmer until berries are soft./Put through a sieve./Reheat and add gelatin to dissolve./Chill, then, if you wish, add red or white wine./Serve ice cold.

*Chef Alfred Georgs,
Museum Restaurant*

Curried Broccoli Soup

"It's worth the time it takes to make this."

Yield: 6 quarts

1 large Spanish onion, diced
7 large cloves garlic, minced
1 stick butter
⅓ cup to ½ cup curry
1 cup water
5 Monga vegetable cubes
1 to 2 tablespoons honey
salt
3 bunches broccoli, trimmed and chopped
 (save the stems)
1½ pounds unpeeled potatoes, diced
¼ pound carrots, peeled and diced
1 bay leaf
1 to 2 tablespoons ginger, grated
1 cinnamon stick
1½ pints half and half

In a stockpot, sauté the onion and garlic in the butter./Add the curry./Cook 5 minutes./Add 1 cup water and continue cooking slowly until mixture is a thick paste./Add the Monga cubes and honey and salt to taste, then the broccoli, potatoes, carrots, bay leaf, ginger, and cinnamon stick./Add water to cover (about 3 quarts) and simmer until vegetables are soft, about 15 or 20 minutes./Add the half and half./Cook another minute or so, remove bay leaf and cinnamon stick, and purée mixture in a food processor.

1 stick butter
2 leeks, thinly sliced
¼ pound celery, cut into matchsticks
1 pound carrots, cut into matchsticks
1 pound mushrooms, sliced
nutmeg

Melt ½ stick butter in a heavy frying pan./ Cook the leeks, celery, broccoli stems, and carrots for 5 minutes./Season with salt and curry if desired./In covered saucepan, cook sliced mushrooms separately in remaining butter until they are soft.

To assemble, combine the purée and vegetable pieces./Season with nutmeg to taste./Serve piping hot.

Mrs. Charles Y. Wadsworth,
Ladies' Committee Associate

South Indian Tomato Rasam

"Spicy hot. Serve after a heavy meal, or with rice as a soup."

Serves 10-12

4 large red tomatoes
3 pints water
2 teaspoons salt, or more
1 teaspoon cumin seed powder
½ teaspoon black pepper
10 cloves garlic
1 tablespoon gingelly oil
 (or Oriental "hot" oil)
⅛ teaspoon mustard seeds
6 fenugreek seeds
1 large onion, sliced
2 dry red chilies, broken into ¼-inch pieces
1 bunch coriander leaves, chopped (or 1
 teaspoon dried)

Wash the tomatoes, boil them with the water and salt until soft, then mash./Grind cumin seeds, pepper, and garlic coarsely, and add to the tomato mixture./Then put a saucepan on low heat, pour in oil, and, when hot, add the mustard and fenugreek seeds./When mustard seeds sputter, add the onions and red chilies, fry a little and then pour them into the tomato mixture./Bring to boiling point, add coriander leaves and remove from heat.

Vishakha Desai, Head of Exhibition
Resources, Public Education

• **Crisp, toasted pumpernickel goes well with soup. Buy unsliced pumpernickel bread and put it in the freezer for an hour or more so that you can slice it wafer thin. Spread with unsalted butter and a light sprinkle of Parmesan cheese. Toast at 325° until crisp.**

ANONYMOUS CHINESE (Ch'ing Dynasty; Ch'ien Lung, 1736–1795)
Pair of Cockerels. Porcelain on gilt-bronze bases
Bequest of Forsyth Wickes; Forsyth Wickes Collection

The Main Dish

Scallops in Wine

"The tastiest scallop dish I have ever enjoyed."
Serves 4-6

2½ pounds bay scallops
1½ cups dry white wine
1 package carrots, shredded
2 bunches celery, cut julienne
salt

Steam scallops in wine for 6-8 minutes./
Remove to warm platter./Save the liquid, and
over it slightly steam the carrots and celery./
Add salt to taste./Place vegetables to side of
scallops./Pour wine sauce over all.

Wine Sauce
1 small onion, grated (or 4 scallions,
  finely minced)
½ cup dry white wine
2 tablespoons water
1 tablespoon white vinegar
¼ cup parsley, finely chopped
1 teaspoon salt
½ teaspoon white pepper

Cook onion in wine, water, vinegar, parsley,
salt, and pepper long enough to reduce liquid
slightly./Pour over scallops and vegetables./
Garnish with parsley sprigs.

Thick Sauce (to be served on the side)
3 large shallots, chopped
1 cup dry white wine
1 tablespoon white vinegar
½ stick butter
½ pint heavy cream
1 teaspoon flour

Cook the shallots in wine and vinegar until
tender./Add butter and melt./Mix the flour
and the cream and whisk in, a little at a time./
Cook over low heat, stirring constantly, until
mixture thickens to consistency of Hollandaise
sauce./Serve separately with the scallop-
vegetable platter.

Mrs. Richard M. Fraser,
Ladies' Committee

Beef and Vegetable Stir-Fry

"This recipe is also wonderful for leftovers,
beef, chicken, lamb, ham, and pork."
Serves 4

All ingredients should be cut the same size
and vegetables should be crisp.
1 tablespoon cornstarch
1 teaspoon sugar
¼ teaspoon ground ginger (or more)
2 tablespoons soy sauce
½ cup beef broth
5 tablespoons salad oil
1 clove garlic, minced or mashed
1 pound boneless lean beef (such as top
  round) sliced about ⅛-inch thick and cut
  into 1 x 2-inch cubes
1 large onion, cut in half, then in
  ¼-inch slices
¼ pound mushrooms, thinly sliced
  through the stems
¾ pound edible-pod peas, with ends and
  strings removed

Mix together cornstarch, sugar, and ginger;
blend in soy and broth; set aside./Heat 2 tablespoons oil over high heat in a wok or large frying pan./When oil is hot add garlic and half of
the beef, stir constantly until meat is lightly
browned, about 2 minutes; turn out onto serving dish./Reheat wok, add 1 tablespoon oil,
and cook remaining meat in the same manner./
turn out onto dish./Add 2 more tablespoons oil
to wok, then onion and mushrooms./Stir and
cook for 2 minutes./Add peas, stir, and cook
for 1 to 2 minutes more./Return meat to pan
and add cornstarch mixture./Stir until sauce
boils and thickens, about 1 minute./Turn out
onto serving dish.

Mrs. John M. Bleakie,
Ladies' Committee Associate

▪ **"That all-softening, overpowering knell,**
The tocsin of the soul, the dinner bell."
Lord Byron

Sole Casserole

"Easy and delicious."

Serves 4-6

6 medium-sized filets of sole
Ritz crackers
Parmesan cheese, grated
½ pint sour cream
½ cup light cream

Grease square casserole./Crumble crackers over bottom to cover well./Wash and dry filets thoroughly./Place layer of them over crackers./Sprinkle on grated cheese./Dilute sour cream with light cream and spread some of it over all./Repeat layers until fish is used up./Finish off with cracker crumbs, cheese, then cream mixture./Dot with butter./Cover tightly with foil./Bake at 325° for 20-25 minutes./Take off foil and bake 10 minutes more at 350°./Serve hot. (Can be frozen, cooked. The day before serving, remove from freezer to defrost./Heat in foil 15 minutes, then uncover and heat as above.)

Mrs. R. Willis Leith, Jr.,
Ladies' Committee

Chicken, Sausage, and Wild Rice Casserole

"A delicious casserole for a buffet."

Serves 8-10

1 pound pork sausage
1 pound mushrooms, sliced
2 medium large onions, sliced
1 (2½-3 pound) chicken (or equivalent in chicken breasts), cooked, boned and cut in bite-size pieces
1 box Uncle Ben's wild rice with herbs and seasonings
¼ cup flour
½ cup heavy or light cream
2½ cups chicken broth

Sauté sausage and set aside./In the fat, sauté mushrooms and onion./Add sausage and chicken./Cook wild rice according to package directions./Mix flour with cream until smooth; add chicken broth and cook until thickened./Season to taste and combine with rice, sausage, chicken, and vegetables./Pour into a baking dish, and bake 25-30 minutes at 350°.

Mrs. Robert H. Cain,
Ladies' Committee Associate

Chicken Scaloppini with Lemon

"A great party dish that can also be used with veal. Can be prepared in less than half an hour (plus baking time)."

Serves 6

3 chicken breasts, boned, skinned, and cut in halves
2 eggs, lightly beaten
½ cup lemon juice
1 cup seasoned bread crumbs
3 tablespoons butter
3 tablespoons oil
6 wafer-thin slices of lemon
6 thin slices of Swiss cheese
1 cup heavy cream

Preheat oven to 350°./Dip chicken in lemon juice, pat with flour, then dip in beaten egg and crumbs./Heat butter and oil in heavy skillet and brown chicken on one side./Remove and place chicken cooked side down in oven-proof baking dish./Cover each piece with a slice of lemon and a slice of cheese./Pour cream over the top and bake about 20-30 minutes until cheese melts and cream bubbles.

Mary Lipscomb Robinson,
Acting Director, Public Education

ADRIAEN BROUWER (Flemish School,
1605/1606 – 1638)
Kitchen Interior. Oil painting
Ernest W. Longfellow Fund

Chicken Breasts Baked with Fresh Tomatoes and Cream

"The fresh tomatoes and cream make this a delicious chicken dish."

Serves 4

½ cup flour
2 teaspoons salt
¼ teaspoon black pepper
2 chicken breasts, cut in half
4-6 tablespoons butter
3 or 4 tomatoes, peeled and sliced thickly
¼ teaspoon tarragon
¼ teaspoon dill
1 cup light cream

Combine flour, salt, and pepper in bag./Add chicken breasts and shake well./Heat butter in skillet to sizzle and brown chicken on both sides./Transfer to casserole./Shake tomato slices in flour mixture and sauté over medium heat until lightly browned./Arrange 6-8 slices around chicken./Break up remaining tomato slices and sprinkle with tarragon and dill./Add 1 tablespoon flour to skillet and stir to blend./Slowly add cream, stirring constantly./Simmer until thickened./Pour sauce over chicken and tomatoes./Cover casserole and bake at 350° for 1 hour, removing cover during last 15 minutes.

Mrs. Albion C. Drinkwater,
Ladies' Committee Associate

▪ *"Here's flowers for you; /Hot lavender, mints savory, marjoram; /The marigold that goes to bed wi' the sun /And with him rises weeping; these are flowers of middle summer..."*
William Shakespeare

Catherine's Whiskey Chicken

"Served by a friend from Singapore. Easy to prepare and elegant."

Serves 4-6

1 chicken, cut in pieces
1 cup heavy cream
2 tablespoons fresh tarragon, chopped
  (or 1 tablespoon dry)
1 cup Scotch whiskey (or less)
½ teaspoon salt
¼ teaspoon pepper

Dip chicken in milk./Put in buttered oven-proof dish; salt lightly./Bake at 350° for 45 minutes to 1 hour./Mix cream, tarragon, and Scotch and pour over chicken./Bake 10-15 minutes longer.

Mrs. Robert G. Hargrove,
Ladies' Committee Associate

Baked Chicken and Beef

"This is so easy to prepare that it is difficult to believe it can be so good."

Serves 4-6

1 (2½-ounce) jar of sliced dried beef*
6 halves boneless chicken breasts
6 bacon strips
1 can cream of mushroom soup
1 cup sour cream
paprika

Place slices of dried beef on bottom of lightly greased casserole dish./Wrap each chicken breast with one strip of bacon and place on top of dried beef./Mix soup and sour cream and cover chicken and beef./Dust with paprika./Bake 3 hours, uncovered, at 275°.

*You may want to soak dried beef in cold water to remove salt.

Mrs. John W. White, Trustee

Bourbon Baked Ham

"A hand-me-down Southern recipe. A poor man's Virginia ham."

Serves 30

1 (16 – 22-pound) precooked ham
1 cup brown sugar
1 tablespoon dry mustard
½ cup Bourbon
lemon slices
whole cloves

Bake ham at 325° for 10-12 minutes per pound./When ham is done and very tender (it may even have pulled away from the bone), remove from oven, cut away any rind, and score deeply in diamond pattern./Pour ⅓ cup Bourbon over ham and return to oven for 15 minutes./Remove from oven and make paste of brown sugar, mustard, and remaining Bourbon./Spread over ham./Decorate by covering entire top surface with thin lemon slices and secure them to ham with whole cloves./Return to oven and bake another ½ hour or so, basting occasionally until lovely and brown./Allow ham to cool a bit and slice thinly across the top./The long baking gets rid of all the water added during processing and avoids "wet"-looking and -tasting ham.

Mrs. John W. Kimball,
Ladies' Committee

Shake 'n Bake Lamb Chops

"Seasoned in this manner, the chops are excellent fare."

Serves 4

3 tablespoons flour
1 teaspoon dry mustard
½ teaspoon salt
⅛ teaspoon pepper
¼ teaspoon oregano
¼ teaspoon basil
8 rib or loin lamb chops, cut 1 inch thick

Mix together in a paper or plastic bag the flour, mustard, salt, pepper, oregano, and basil./Add lamb chops 2 at a time and shake until well coated./Broil 3 or 4 inches from heat, about 7 minutes on each side or until cooked as you like it.

Mrs. William E. Park,
Ladies' Committee Associate

Lamb with Dill Sauce

"A favorite winter dish, handed down from my Swedish grandmothers, used for many years by my Swedish-American mother, and even my Polish-Italian husband likes it!"

Serves 6

3 pounds lamb (any cut, preferably boned)
1 quart boiling water (or to cover)
1 tablespoon dill seed, or dill weed (dried),
  or sprigs of fresh dill
2 teaspoons salt
pepper
3 or 4 tablespoons butter
5 tablespoons flour
1 cup milk (or sour cream)
salt and pepper

Cut lamb into pieces as for stew, removing all possible fat./Brown on all sides in large skillet./Add boiling water, dill, salt, and pepper./Cover tightly and simmer 1½ hours, or until lamb is tender./Remove meat from stock to serving dish and keep warm./Strain stock and skim off fat./Use stock for sauce./Melt butter and stir in flour, salt, and pepper./Add lamb stock, stirring to prevent lumping, adding milk (or sour cream), and stirring slowly until mixture thickens./Add sauce to meat in casserole serving dish (or return meat to sauce, briefly, to make sure meat is warmed through; do not let it come to a boil)./Serve with small boiled potatoes, sprinkled with dill or parsley and drizzled with melted butter.

Mrs. C. Vincent Vappi,
Overseer

Butterflied Lamb

"A dinner party favorite."

Serves 8-10

Marinade
4 tablespoons lemon juice
4 tablespoons soy sauce
2 tablespoons honey
1 tablespoon red wine vinegar
6 large pieces candied ginger, diced
3 cloves garlic, crushed
¼ cup sherry
8 (3-inch) sprigs rosemary
   (leaves cut from stems)
1 (8-pound) leg of lamb, butterflied
   (Have butcher remove all fat and skin.)

Marinate lamb 24 hours, turning it over whenever you open the refrigerator door./Place lamb on broiler and pour half the marinade over it./Broil 4 inches from heat 6-10 minutes on a side for rare, longer for well done./The time varies with temperature of the broiler./Turn meat and pour over remainder of marinade./Remove meat to cutting board and pour marinade from broiler pan over it./Baked potatoes and peas are a good accompaniment.

Mrs. George N. Proctor,
Ladies' Committee Associate

Lamb with Spinach, Avgolemono

"A Greek family recipe."

Serves 6

3 pounds lean shoulder of lamb
2-3 tablespoons butter
2-3 onions, chopped
1 cup water
salt and pepper
3 pounds spinach
3 eggs
2 tablespoons flour
juice of 1½ lemons

Cut lamb into 2-inch cubes./Melt butter in large pot, add meat and onions, and brown well over moderate heat./Add water and salt and pepper./Bring mixture to a boil; cover and simmer for an hour./Wash spinach thoroughly and remove any tough stalks./Add spinach to meat and continue cooking for 15 minutes./Remove from heat and allow mixture to cool slightly while preparing avgolemono sauce: beat eggs until light, add flour and lemon juice, and mix well./Very slowly add liquid from stew, stirring constantly until about 1 cup of the hot liquid has been added./Pour egg mixture into stew, slowly shaking pan until sauce mixes with liquid in stew./Serve immediately. (Don't make sauce until ready to serve.)

Mrs. George D. Mason,
Ladies' Committee Associate

Oriental Baked Chicken

"One of our favorite chicken dishes."

Serves 4-6

1 frying chicken, skin removed, cut in pieces
½ cup soy sauce
½ cup sugar
1 cup dry red burgundy
1 teaspoon ground ginger
2 cloves garlic, crushed

Sauté the chicken in butter to brown lightly./Arrange the pieces in a baking dish./Mix the rest of the ingredients and heat just long enough to dissolve the sugar./Pour over the chicken./Cover with foil./Bake at 350° about 1 hour.

Mrs. Sylvester B. Kelley,
Ladies' Committee Associate

Indonesian Meatballs

"These meatballs are very good as appetizers with drinks. They also freeze well."

Serves 6-8

¾ cup potato flakes or buds
2 large eggs
½ cup milk
1 small onion, finely chopped
2 cloves garlic, finely chopped
4 teaspoons curry powder
pepper and salt (do not oversalt; soy sauce in gravy will make the meatballs saltier)
½ teaspoon Worcestershire sauce
2 pounds ground beef
8 tablespoons dried grated coconut, unsweetened (available in Middle- or Far-Eastern food stores)
2-3 tablespoons salad oil for browning
4 tablespoons soy sauce, plus 2 cups water

In a large bowl mix potato flakes, eggs, milk, onion, garlic, curry, salt, pepper and Worcestershire sauce./Let stand for a few minutes until flakes have absorbed liquids./Add ground beef and coconut./Mix well./Form meatballs the size of a large marble./Heat oil in large frying pan or wok./Brown the meatballs all around in one layer in several batches./When all the meatballs are browned pour off some of the fat./Add the soy sauce and water to the pan and scrape the bottom and sides thoroughly./Bring to a boil and add all the browned meatballs./Simmer for at least 10 minutes (or up to 1 hour)./Turn regularly.

Serve with boiled rice, green beans, cucumber salad, green salad, chutney, and Indonesian Sambal (hot pepper condiment).

Mrs. Jan Fontein,
wife of the Director

Hawaiian Meat Balls

"Wonderful as an hors d'oeuvre or main course."

Serves 4-6

1½ pounds ground beef
2 eggs
1½ cups Italian seasoned bread crumbs
2 eggs
¼ cup vinegar (wine or garlic flavored)
2 teaspoons Worcestershire sauce
¼ cup catsup
1 teaspoon garlic salt

Combine all ingredients and shape into balls about 1½-2 inches in diameter./Brown meatballs in a little fat in large skillet./Pour off any excess fat when browned, then cover with sauce and simmer 20-30 minutes.

Sauce
1 (29-ounce) can pineapple chunks
2 tablespoons cornstarch
¼ cup vinegar
¼ cup brown sugar
2 tablespoons soy sauce
1 cup green pepper, chopped

Drain syrup from pineapple chunks and add enough water to make 1 cup./In saucepan, mix syrup and water with cornstarch, vinegar, brown sugar, and soy sauce and heat until clear and thick./Add pineapple chunks and green pepper./Serve with rice as a main dish or in a chafing dish as an *hors d'oeuvre.*

Mrs. Richard C. Anderson,
Ladies' Committee

▪ **"Small cheer and great welcome make a merry feast."**

William Shakespeare

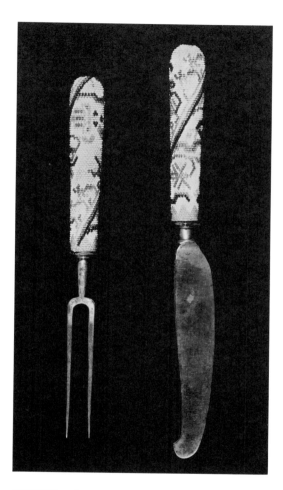

FRENCH, 18th century
Knife and fork. Steel with beadwork handles
Elizabeth Day McCormick Collection

Roast Loin of Pork

"A delicious, inexpensive dinner party favorite."

Serves 8

4-5 pound boneless loin of pork
3 tablespoons flour
½ tablespoon salt
2 teaspoons pepper
1 teaspoon sage
¾ teaspoon marjoram
1 clove garlic, chopped
½ cup apple cider
1 cup beef broth

Rub meat with combined flour, salt, pepper, sage, and marjoram./Place on wire rack in roasting pan./Add garlic, cider, and broth./ Bake 30 minutes at 425°, reduce heat to 325°, bake 1 hour and 20 minutes longer./Baste occasionally, adding broth if needed./Let roast stand 10 minutes before carving.

Pan Sauce
2 tablespoons flour
1 teaspoon Dijon mustard
1½ tablespoons catsup
1 cup applesauce
2 teaspoons horseradish
1 cup beef broth
1 cup water
½ teaspoon salt
1 or 2 ounces Calvados or applejack

Spoon off excess fat./Stir in flour and cook over medium heat for 3 minutes./Add remaining ingredients and heat thoroughly./Remove from heat and add Calvados or applejack./ Serve sauce in sauceboat.

Mrs. John A. Pooley,
Ladies' Committee

Hamburger Casserole

"A different approach to cabbage."

Serves 10-12

2 pounds of hamburger
1 large onion, chopped
1 teaspoon cinnamon
½ teaspoon cloves
1 large can stewed tomatoes
1 (8-ounce) can tomato sauce
1 large green cabbage, chopped
lemon juice
salt

Brown hamburger and onion, then add cinnamon, cloves, stewed tomatoes, and tomato sauce./Spread the bottom of a 4-quart casserole or baking dish with one half of the cabbage./Add a layer of the meat mixture, then a layer of the chopped cabbage and over all the remainder of the meat mixture./Sprinkle a bit of lemon juice over the surface./Bake at 350° for 40 minutes.

Mrs. Frederick L. Good, Jr.,
Ladies' Committee Associate

Beautiful Three-Way Bluefish

"This is my favorite dish because it is delicious, versatile, and always gets raves and requests for the recipe."

Serves many for cocktails
Serves 6 for luncheon

2 pounds bluefish fillets (all skin removed)
1½ cups sour cream
¾ cup mayonnaise
1 teaspoon celery salt
1 teaspoon dill weed
¼ teaspoon thyme
¼ teaspoon basil
¼ teaspoon pepper
sprigs of fresh dill

Place bluefish in shallow baking dish./Combine other ingredients and spread three quarters of mixture over fish./Sprinkle with fresh dill./Bake at 350° for approximately 35 minutes./Cool in refrigerator./Do not pour off any liquid, as this forms a delicious jelly when cold.

Frost with remaining sour cream mixture and decorate with fresh dill./Serve with melba rounds for *hors d'oeuvres* or on lettuce for luncheon.

Mrs. Samuel S. Rogers,
Ladies' Committee Associate

Mum's New England Salt Fish Dinner

"Coastal New England meal from the sea and land. Filling and delicious on a cold blustery day."

Serves 6

1 pound box salt codfish
½ pound salt pork
3 tablespoons flour
2 cups milk
2 hard-cooked eggs
6 large potatoes, baked
2 cups cooked beets, sliced or diced
and buttered

Soak salt codfish overnight./Cook according to package directions./Dice salt pork and fry until crisp./In a saucepan combine 2 tablespoons of liquid pork fat and flour./Stir in milk and cook until thickened./Chop hard-cooked eggs and stir into sauce./Let each guest prepare his own plate./Open potato and spread with butter./Cover with hot salt codfish./Top this with buttered beets./Ladle egg sauce on top and garnish with pork scraps.

Mrs. Richard H. Overholt,
Ladies' Committee Associate

Stolen Shrimp Casserole

"Worth stealing!"

Serves 4-6

1 pound small shrimp
4 stalks celery, cut in small cubes
1 (4-ounce) jar pimientos, sliced
1 (8-ounce) can water chestnuts, sliced
½ pound Swiss cheese, grated
2 (10¾-ounce) cans undiluted cream of
   shrimp soup
¼ cup scallions, chopped

Mix all together./Place in casserole./Bake at
350° for 1 hour./Serve over rice. (Cook rice in
tightly covered oven-proof container in the
oven at the same time to conserve energy.)

Mrs. Richard G. Scheide,
Ladies' Committee

Bohemian Oysters

"Good buffet or gala supper fare."

Serves 12-15

4 dozen oysters
½ pound noodles (preferably green)
1 pint oyster liquor
1 pint half and half
2 egg yolks
2 tablespoons cornstarch
1 cup butter, softened
1 tablespoon Kitchen Bouquet
dash of Tabasco
1 pound mild cheese, grated
salt and pepper

Drain oysters./Cook in hot skillet, scraping up
the scorched juice and bits./Season with salt
and continue cooking for about 5 minutes./
Add oyster liquor and half and half./When
this is hot, add egg yolks, cornstarch, and butter, creamed together./Add Kitchen Bouquet
and Tabasco./Cook until thick and creamy./
Cook noodles according to package
directions./Layer the oysters, cooked noodles,
and grated cheese alternately in very large casserole, ending with the cheese./Heat at 350°
only until heated through; too long will dry it.

Mrs. John Lee Potter,
Ladies' Committee Associate

Ken Roberts's Swordfish

*"Mr. Roberts introduced this to my mother when
I was a little girl. It was years before I realized
others enjoy swordfish served any other way."*

Broil swordfish steaks at high heat very
briefly, 4 to 5 minutes./To serve, allow each
guest to add Worcestershire sauce and light
cream, preferably in that order./For years,
we've had discussions about cream first or
Worcestershire./Either way it's gorgeous.

Mrs. Richard H. Overholt,
Ladies' Committee Associate

Last-Minute Shrimp Dish

"Fast, easy, and delicious!"

Line buttered casserole with raw shrimp,
cleaned and deveined./Sprinkle generously
with lemon juice, dash of Worcestershire
sauce, and vermouth (amount depending on
number of shrimp you are cooking)./Cover
shrimp with seasoned bread crumbs or stuffing
mix, drizzle with melted butter. (If desired,
add minced shallots or garlic to melted
butter.)/Bake at 375° until crumbs brown,
about 15 minutes./Serve with rice.

Mrs. John B. Sears,
Ladies' Committee

Pork Strips in Black Bean Sauce

"Best made in a wok but you may substitute an electric skillet."

Serves 4

4 (4-ounce) pork cutlets
2 tablespoons black bean sauce
1 clove garlic, crushed
2 tablespoons sherry
2-3 slices fresh ginger root
peanut oil for frying
1 clove garlic, sliced
1 medium onion, sliced
2 tablespoons sunflower seeds

Cut pork across the grain into thin strips./ Combine bean sauce, garlic, sherry, and ginger root in large bowl./Toss the pork in marinade, then let stand for at least an hour./ Remove from marinade and stir-fry in wok (or electric skillet) in 1-2 tablespoons of peanut oil, seasoned with 1 or 2 slices of garlic./When pork is nearly done, add onions and sunflower seeds as well as any remaining marinade./ Continue to stir-fry for 1-2 minutes./Serve with stir-fried seasonal vegetables.

Margaret Leveque,
Conservation Intern, Textiles

Haddock Stuffed with Oysters

"Delicious served with French bread and spinach salad."

Serves 6

3 pounds haddock (or cod) fillets
2 teaspoons lemon juice
salt to taste
½-1 pint oysters
1 egg, slightly beaten
1 cup bread crumbs
¼ cup butter, melted

paprika
Hollandaise sauce
lemon wedges and parsley

Brush fish with lemon juice./Sprinkle lightly with salt./Place half of fish in bottom of buttered baking dish./Cover with oysters./Top with remaining fish./Brush top of fillet with some of beaten egg./Mix bread crumbs with butter, plus generous dash of paprika, and sprinkle over fish./Bake uncovered for 30-35 minutes at 350°./Serve with Hollandaise sauce./Garnish with lemon wedges and parsley.

Mrs. George N. Proctor,
Ladies' Committee Associate

Chicken Monique

"I have never served this without receiving many comments and requests for the recipe. May be done ahead and frozen."

Serves 6

6 chicken breasts, boned and skinned
flour, paprika
butter
½-1 cup dry sherry
3 teaspoons cornstarch
1½ cups heavy cream (or half and half)
1 cup white wine or vermouth
1½ cups imported Swiss cheese, grated
salt and pepper

Mix flour and paprika./Coat chicken with the mixture./Fry chicken in butter until brown./ Add sherry./Cover and simmer for 20 minutes.Remove chicken to a shallow casserole./Mix cornstarch, cream, and wine; add to chicken and stir./Top with the cheese. Bake at 350° for 35-45 minutes.

A tossed salad and French bread complete the meal.

Mrs. Franklin W. Hobbs,
Ladies' Committee Associate

J.B.S. CHARDIN (French, 1699–1779)
Kitchen Table. Oil painting
Gift of Mrs. Peter Chardon Brooks

Chicken Chardin

"Served at a 1979 Patron's Dinner preceding the opening of the Chardin exhibition."

Serves 8-10

**8-10 servings of boned chicken breasts and
  thighs
8 strips bacon, cut in ¼-inch pieces
4 ounces ham, cut into 1½ x ¼-inch strips
½ teaspoon black peppercorns, crushed
4 bay leaves
6 cloves
2 medium onions, cut into 1½-inch sticks
2 cucumbers, peeled and cut lengthwise into
  1½-inch sticks
1 quart chicken broth
½ bottle red Burgundy
cornstarch
parsley**

Brown the chicken either in a pan or under the broiler./Place in a casserole./Sauté the bacon and ham. To the bacon fat, add the pepper-corns, bay leaves, cloves, and onions./Cook slowly until the onions are limp./Add the cucumber; sauté and pour the mixture over the chicken./Add chicken broth and red Burgundy to cover the chicken./Cover, bring to a boil, simmer about 10 minutes or until chicken is tender./Pour off the liquid into a cooking pot and thicken slightly with a little cornstarch mixed with a little red wine./Season with additional salt if needed, bring to a boil, and pour over the chicken and vegetables./Garnish with chopped parsley./Serve with rice or boiled potatoes.

*Chef Alfred Georgs,
Museum Restaurant*

Veal with Mustard Sauce

"An unusual and delicious way with veal."

Serves 4

**1 pound veal scallops, pounded thin
⅓ cup flour
salt and pepper
6 tablespoons butter
2 tablespoons shallots, minced (or 1
  tablespoon dried green onions)
½ cup dry white wine
1 cup cream
2 tablespoons Dijon or Dusseldorf mustard**

Pound scaloppine thin if they are not sliced thin./Blend flour with salt and pepper and dredge meat on both sides./Heat butter in large heavy skillet until hot but not brown./Cook scaloppine quickly (about 2 minutes on each side)./Remove to a platter and keep warm.

Add shallots to skillet and cook briefly, stirring./Add wine and cook, stirring until it is almost evaporated./Add the cream and boil it up, stirring./Cook about 30 seconds and turn off heat./Stir in the mustard./Do not cook further./Spoon sauce over veal./Serve with buttered noodles.

*Mrs. George W. Ferguson,
Ladies' Committee*

Chicken Kiev

"A dish that has been around for a long time but one my guests rave about each time. Can be made in the morning and fried at the last min-ute while the pilaf cooks."

Serves 4 generously for
dinner; 8 for luncheon

**8 single chicken breasts, boned and skinned
1½ sticks butter
2 teaspoons lemon juice**

½ teaspoon salt
⅛ teaspoon white pepper
2 tablespoons fresh parsley, minced
1 tablespoon shallots, minced
½ teaspoon dried tarragon
¾ cup flour
2 eggs beaten with salt, pepper, 2 teaspoons
   water, and 1 teaspoon oil
peanut oil

Pound each chicken breast between pieces of waxed paper until it is ¼ inch thick./This may be done 24 hours ahead and the breasts refrigerated between layers of waxed paper.

Soften the butter in a mixer and gradually add lemon juice, salt, pepper, parsley, shallots, and tarragon./On a piece of waxed paper form a 4 x 3-inch rectangle with this mixture and chill./Cut into 8 pieces, each 3 inches long, and keep chilled until ready to use.

Put a finger of butter along the largest edge of the breast./Roll the breast, tucking in the ends with your fingers./Press the meat together on all sides to enclose the butter completely.

Line up 3 plates, one with flour, one with beaten eggs, and one with bread crumbs./One by one, roll the chicken pieces first in the flour, then the egg mixture, and finally in crumbs, making sure that the crumbs cover the entire surface of the chicken./Refrigerate for at least an hour in order to set the crumbs.

Heat the peanut oil to 375° in a deep fryer or a deep pan./Fry the breasts 4 at a time for 5 minutes./Drain on paper towels in a 200° oven until all the pieces are done./Serve immediately.

Baby carrots tossed in butter, rice pilaf, and simple green salad are good accompaniments.

(Warn your guests of the impending dramatic spurt of butter when they cut into the chicken or you will be sending their clothes to the cleaner!)

Mrs. Malcolm L. Trayser,
Ladies' Committee Associate

Matrosen of Beef

"This is an excellent dish for company as it is not too heavy but is delicious."

Serves 4

1½ pounds lean stew meat
1½ tablespoons oil (or part olive oil,
   part salad oil)
1 medium onion, peeled and sliced
1 tablespoon wine vinegar
½ cup red wine
½ teaspoon anchovy paste
1 bay leaf
¼ teaspoon dried thyme
1 clove garlic, peeled and crushed
1 medium carrot, grated
1 medium apple, peeled and grated
1 stalk celery, diced
pinch of pepper, freshly ground
½ cup beef consommé (canned, undiluted)
½ teaspoon salt

Sear meat in oil, remove from pan, and lightly brown onions in drippings./Add vinegar, wine, anchovy paste, bay leaf, thyme, and garlic./Bring to a boil, return meat, cover and simmer for ½ hour./Meanwhile, sauté carrot, apple, and celery in ½ tablespoon oil for 5 minutes, stirring./Add vegetables to meat with pepper and consommé./Cover and bake at 325° for 1½ hours./Season with salt./Serve with poppy seed noodles, rice, or pilaf.

Mrs. Kevit R. Cook,
Ladies' Committee Associate

▪ **"Better die of good wine and good company than of slow disease and doctor's doses."**
William Makepeace Thackeray

HENRY SARGENT (American, 1770–1845)
The Dinner Party. Oil painting
Gift of Mrs. Horatio A. Lamb in memory of Mr. and
Mrs. Winthrop Sargent

Fishmonger, 1750–1758. Chelsea porcelain
Gift of Richard C. Paine

Quick Steamed Fish

"For those with a microwave oven."

For each 1 pound of fish fillets:
¼ cup onion, chopped
⅛ cup green pepper, chopped
½ cup celery and celery tops, chopped
2 tablespoons oil or butter
½ cup tomatoes, chopped
dry white wine
generous pinch of tarragon and dill, or a
**   combination of both**
salt, pepper, and paprika
⅓ cup Romano cheese, grated

In oven-proof deep dish, on stove top or under broiler, braise onions, green pepper, celery and celery tops in oil or butter./Remove from stove and add chopped tomatoes./Place cleaned fish fillets on top of vegetables./Sprinkle with dry wine, herbs, salt, pepper and paprika./Cover generously with cheese./Cover dish with plastic wrap and cook on high in microwave oven for 3-4 minutes, turning dish at least once during cooking.

Leslie Melville Smith,
Department of Textiles

Fish on Skewers

"This works best with swordfish but is good with halibut too."

Cut fish in chunks about 1½ x 1 inch./Marinate for a few hours in the following mixture:

3 parts oil
1 part fresh lemon juice
2 parts vermouth
pinch of oregano
a little or a lot of garlic
a few slices of onion
salt

Skewer fish and broil about 8-10 minutes, turning once and basting.

Mrs. Selwyn A. Kudisch,
Ladies' Committee

PIETER BRUEGHEL (Netherlandish, ca. 1525–1569)
Fat Kitchen. Engraving
Babcock Bequest

Unusual Vegetable Dishes

Carrot Casserole

"A great 'second' vegetable for a hungry family during winter."

Serves 6-8

3 cups carrots, sliced and cooked
¼ cup cheddar cheese, grated
1 medium onion, diced
¾ cup Ritz crackers, crushed
3 tablespoons butter, melted
salt and pepper
¾ cup carrot juice

Mix all together in casserole; pour carrot juice on top./Heat 20 minutes at 375°.

Mrs. Edward Kenerson,
Ladies' Committee

Carrot and Mushroom Mold

"This makes a delicious vegetable accompaniment for lamb, fish, or chicken."

Serves 4

1 pound young carrots, scraped and very
** thinly sliced**
2 tablespoons butter
1 cup chicken stock
½ teaspoon sugar
1 teaspoon salt
⅛ teaspoon white pepper
1 teaspoon olive oil
¼ pound mushrooms, rinsed, trimmed,
** and minced**
½ shallot, minced
3 eggs
4 tablespoons heavy cream
4 tablespoons Swiss Gruyère cheese, grated
2 tablespoons fresh chervil or parsley,
** chopped**

Heat the butter in a heavy-bottomed saucepan; add the carrots and let them color without browning, cooking for about 10 minutes./Then add the chicken stock, sugar, salt, and pepper./

Simmer the carrots uncovered until they have absorbed all of the liquid (about 20 minutes)./ The carrots should not be dry.

In a skillet place the olive oil and sauté the minced mushrooms and shallot./Remove the carrots to a chopping board and chop them until relatively fine. (Or use a food processor.)/ With a fork beat the eggs lightly in a bowl, add the heavy cream, carrots, mushrooms, Swiss cheese, and chervil./Mix together gently./ Using a small decorative mold, brush it lightly with butter, and put in the carrot and mushroom mixture./Cover the mold with aluminum foil and bake at 425° in a pan of hot water for 45-50 minutes or until the carrots are completely set./Unmold on a platter and garnish with sprigs of parsley or chervil.

Anne L. Poulet,
Curator, European Decorative Arts

Shredded Carrots Lyonnaise

"No water to drain away the flavor of fresh carrots."

Serves 6

2 tablespoons butter
1 small onion, chopped
1 pound carrots, peeled and shredded in
** food processor**
2 tablespoons fresh parsley, finely chopped

Over medium-low heat, simmer onion in butter in heavy saucepan until it is translucent but not browned./Add carrots; stir once and reduce heat to a very low simmer./Cover and cook for approximately 20 minutes, until carrots are tender./Stir in chopped parsley and serve./Try without salt first; if carrots are fresh, they will not need additional seasoning./ May be made ahead and reheated.

Larry Salmon,
Former Curator, Textiles

Cabbage Cybèle

"Colorful and easy way to use summer vegetables."

Serves 6

½ stick butter
1 small young head of cabbage, cut in ½-inch squares
1 red pepper, cut in ½-inch squares
1 (9-inch) zucchini, unpeeled and cut in ¼-inch slices
salt and pepper

Melt butter in a large skillet./Sauté cabbage, pepper, and zucchini together until tender and crisp./Season to taste and serve piping hot.

Mrs. George N. Proctor,
Ladies' Committee Associate

Mushroom Dish

"Delicious with roast beef; good buffet dish."

Serves 8 or 20

For 8:
1 pound mushrooms
10 slices bread
½ stick butter, melted
salt and pepper
1½ cups heavy cream

For 20:
5 pounds mushrooms
1 large loaf bread
½ pound butter
salt and pepper
3½ pints heavy cream

Butter large casserole dish./Toast bread and remove crusts./Butter generously, cut into squares./Alternate layers of toasted bread with mushrooms, ending with large mushrooms on top. (Salt and pepper lightly as you go along.)/Pour over heavy cream./Refrigerate overnight./Bake uncovered at 350° for 1 hour.

Mrs. William E. Park,
Ladies' Committee Associate

Skillet Hawaiian Vegetables

"A taste of the Islands."

Serves 8

4 tablespoons butter or margarine
10 large mushrooms, sliced
1 cup green pepper, coarsely chopped
1 cup onion, diced
1 (13½-ounce) can pineapple chunks
6 large carrots, sliced diagonally
¼ teaspoon basil
¼ teaspoon curry (optional)
¼ teaspoon ground ginger
1 tablespoon brown sugar
1 (8½-ounce) can water chestnuts, drained and sliced

Melt 3 tablespoons butter in skillet, add mushrooms and green pepper, and sauté./Remove from pan and set aside./Melt last tablespoon of butter in skillet and cook onions until golden./Drain pineapple, reserving syrup./Add pineapple syrup, carrots, basil, curry, ginger, and brown sugar to onions./Simmer 35 minutes or until carrots are tender./Add mushrooms, green pepper, pineapple, and water chestnuts./Cook 5 minutes longer.

Carol Howard,
Gallery Instructor

Zippy Carrots

"This is a sauce to add to boiled carrots to give them a special touch."

Serves 4

cooked carrots
2 tablespoons butter, melted and mixed with:
¼ cup brown sugar
2 tablespoons Grey Poupon mustard
¼ teaspoon salt

Pour over drained carrots and, just before serving, top with chopped parsley.

Mrs. Henry F. Cate, Jr.,
Ladies' Committee Associate

Grated Carrots and Parsnips

"A happy blend of vegetables."

Serves 10-12

1 stick butter
⅛ cup sugar (or less)
1 pound carrots, grated
1 pound parsnips, grated
¼ cup white wine
salt and pepper

Melt butter and sugar in a large frying pan; add rest of ingredients./Stir until well blended; cover and cook over medium heat for about 5 minutes, stirring several times./Cook until done but still crisp.

Mrs. James M. Sampson,
Ladies' Committee Associate

Curried Tomatoes

"A good way to use those not-too-flavorful winter tomatoes. Simple, quick, and very good."

Serves 6-8

1 teaspoon onion, chopped
2 tablespoons butter
6 tomatoes, sliced
1 cup cream
1 tablespoon flour
1 teaspoon curry powder
salt
dash of cayenne

Heat onion in butter in a large skillet./Add tomatoes and cook until just tender, while making a paste of cream, flour, curry powder, salt, and cayenne to taste./Remove tomatoes to platter and keep warm./Pour cream mixture into skillet and stir until it thickens./Pour over tomatoes./Serve on hot buttered toast for luncheon or over pasta as a dinner dish.

Mrs. John Lee Potter,
Ladies' Committee Associate

Orange Cups with Yams

"An old southern dish from my southern cook. Excellent with duck or ham."

Serves 12

4 (1-pound) cans yams
12 large oranges
¼ pound butter
½-¾ cup light brown sugar
    (according to taste)
cinnamon
nutmeg

Wash oranges, cut in half, remove pulp and seeds and as much membrane as possible./Pour juice from pulp into container for another use./Drain yams; mash and add butter, sugar, and spice./Heat, but do *not* cook./Gently mix orange pulp with yams./Pile *hot* mixture into orange cups./Place under broiler until golden brown.

Mrs. Henry E. Foley,
Ladies' Committee Associate

Spinach Casserole

"This recipe doubles or triples magnificently. It is enormously popular at a buffet. Never any left over!"

Serves 16

4 packages frozen chopped spinach
8 ounces cream cheese
¼ cup butter
salt and pepper, freshly ground
1 cup bread stuffing mix
½ teaspoon sage

Thaw spinach and drain well./Mix spinach with cheese, 1 tablespoon butter, salt, and pepper./Stir to mix and pour into 1½-quart casserole dish./Melt remaining butter./Toss with bread crumbs and sage./Sprinkle mixture over spinach./Bake at 350° for 20-30 minutes, until bubbly and brown.

Mrs. F. Thomas Westcott,
Ladies' Committee

Zucchini au Gratin

"This is an especially quick dish for me as I prepare the zucchini and onions in a microwave oven."

Serves 4-6

2 pounds zucchini
2 medium onions, chopped
2 tablespoons butter or margarine
8 ounces sharp cheddar cheese, grated
3 eggs, slightly beaten
salt and pepper

Slice zucchini (do not peel) into ½-inch slices and steam or simmer until half done./Sauté chopped onion in butter or margarine./Lay zucchini slices in a large flat casserole and sprinkle over them sautéed onion./Mix cheese with eggs, salt, and pepper, spread over the zucchini and onions, and bake at 350° for about 30 minutes or until firm around the edges and browned on top.

Mrs. Emerson T. Oliver,
Ladies' Committee Associate

My Mother-in-Law's Zucchini and Artichoke Heart Casserole

"Delicious and different from other zucchini dishes."

Serves 4-6

1-2 cloves fresh garlic, minced
1 small onion, minced
½ green pepper, diced
3-4 tablespoons salad oil
1 (8½-ounce) can artichoke hearts, rinsed,
  drained, and quartered
1-2 small zucchini, scrubbed and sliced horizontally
½ teaspoon salt
¼ teaspoon pepper
¼ cup Parmesan cheese, grated

Brown garlic, onion, and pepper in hot oil./Set aside./In same oil quickly sauté the artichoke hearts and zucchini./Add salt and pepper.Return garlic mixture to pan and mix well./Transfer to an oven-proof dish, sprinkle with cheese, and heat at 350° for 5-10 minutes or until cheese melts slightly and sticks to the vegetables.

Sarah Lumsden,
Coordinator for Planned Giving,
Resource Development

Green Beans Lucretia

"Easy and the sauce can be done ahead."

Serves 3-4

1 pound green beans, cooked
Sauce
6 tablespoons water
2 tablespoons butter
1 teaspoon cornstarch
1½ teaspoons soy sauce
1 (8-ounce) can water chestnuts, sliced

Bring water, butter, cornstarch, and soy sauce to a boil to thicken./Add water chestnuts and pour over beans.

Mrs. Everett Black,
Ladies' Committee Associate

- **Plunge green vegetables into ice-cold water after cooking to retain the green color; reheat quickly before serving.**

- **Peeled potatoes will be whiter and more mealy if placed in cold water overnight before cooking.**

- **Sliced water chestnuts added to cooked French-style beans add a nice crunch.**

- **A good pinch of dried dill added to cooked lima beans gives zip.**

Peperonata (Stewed Peppers)

"A continental recipe that makes good use of plentiful harvest vegetables."

Serves 4-6

2 pounds large green, red, and yellow sweet
peppers
¼-½ cup Bertolli olive oil
2 medium onions, thinly sliced
1 pound tomatoes, fresh or canned
basil leaves, fresh or dried
salt
pepper, freshly ground

Wash peppers; cut them open and remove seeds, white membrane, and core./Cut into 1-inch strips./In an earthenware casserole sauté thinly sliced onion with oil; add peppers, chopped tomatoes, basil leaves, salt, and pepper./Cover the casserole and cook slowly for about an hour, stirring from time to time./If the liquid is too much at the end, reduce it by taking the lid off and raising the flame./Serve the peppers hot or cold.

Variation: zucchini and eggplant cut into pieces may be substituted or can be cooked with the peppers.

Mrs. Carlos H. Tosi,
Ladies' Committee Associate

Hungarian Cabbage Noodles

"An unusual and delicious change from potatoes or rice."

Serves 8-10

1 firm, solid head of white cabbage, chopped
1 heaping tablespoon coarse salt
1 large onion, chopped
1 stick butter
salt and pepper
1 package wide noodles

Chop cabbage and place in large bowl./ Sprinkle with heaping tablespoon coarse salt./ Set flat plate on bowl and weight to draw out liquid from cabbage./Let it stand a few hours and squeeze *as dry as possible.*

Sauté chopped onion in butter until golden./ Add cabbage and sauté the cabbage quickly to brown, then cover and cook until cabbage is tender, stirring frequently./Add salt and pepper to taste.

Cook noodles according to directions on package./Drain./Add butter if you wish./Mix cabbage mixture into drained noodles (we like noodles on firm side)./Keep hot and serve as a pasta course or with meat entrée as a side dish. (Sautéed cabbage may be made ahead of time and frozen.)

Mrs. Paul Bernat, Trustee

Cheese Potato Crisps

"Crisp like French fries but so much better!"

Serves 5-6

¼ cup butter
5 medium potatoes, peeled
1½ cups Cornflakes, crushed
¾ cup sharp American cheese, shredded
1½ teaspoons salt
¾ teaspoon paprika

Melt butter in jelly-roll pan in 375° oven./Cut potatoes in lengthwise slices about ¼ inch thick; arrange in single layer in pan, turning once to coat both sides with butter./Combine Cornflakes, cheese, salt, and paprika; sprinkle over potatoes./Bake at 375° for 25-30 minutes or until topping is lightly browned and crisp.

Mrs. Joseph A. Valatka,
Ladies' Committee Associate

• **Cook frozen peas with a pinch of dried mint**
and a pinch of sugar to bring out a just-
picked flavor.

Super Spinach

"This recipe can be multiplied and cooked in large lasagna pans for a big party."

Serves 8

2 packages frozen chopped spinach
2 eggs
½ cup milk
¼ cup flour
nutmeg, grated
¼ pound sharp cheddar cheese, grated
1 tablespoon chives, chopped
salt and pepper

Defrost spinach and drain thoroughly./In a 2-quart casserole beat eggs and milk lightly./ Add spinach, sprinkle with flour, and stir./ Add generous grating of nutmeg, grated cheese, chives, salt, and pepper to taste; stir gently./Bake 20-30 minutes at 325°.

Mrs. Peter Brooke,
Ladies' Committee Associate

• **Spread peeled, sliced eggplant with mayonnaise; coat with bread crumbs and Parmesan cheese. Bake at 450° for 15 minutes.**

Very Special Creamed Onions

"A Robinson family favorite."

Serves 6

2 dozen small to medium white onions, peeled
¼ cup butter
¼ cup flour
½ teaspoon salt
fresh pepper
1 cup chicken broth
1 cup light cream
3 tablespoons Parmesan cheese, grated
1 tablespoon parsley, chopped
3 tablespoons pimiento strips

In a large saucepan, cover onions with boiling water./Simmer over moderate heat until tender (about 30 minutes)./Drain well./Melt butter in medium saucepan; blend in flour, salt, and pepper, stirring constantly until thick and smooth./Stir in cheese and parsley./Remove from heat./Add onions and pour into 1½-quart casserole./Bake covered 10-15 minutes at 350°, stirring once./Arrange pimiento strips on top and bake 10 minutes more until bubbly.

Mary Lipscomb Robinson,
Acting Director, Public Education

ANONYMOUS FRENCH, 15th century
People Picnicking. Woodcut from a Book of Hours, 1498 (Paris: Pigouchet)
Maria Antoinette Evans Fund

Mexican Corn Pudding

"Serve this as a luncheon dish, as a meat accompaniment, or pour it into a pie shell and turn it into a quiche."

Serves 8-10

2 medium onions, chopped
1½ cups butter, melted
3 eggs, beaten
1 cup heavy cream
½ cup buttermilk
1 cup yellow cornmeal
1½ cups cooked fresh or frozen corn
1½ tablespoons Jalapeño pepper, chopped
2 cups cheese, grated (half Monterey Jack
   and half sharp cheddar)

Gently sauté onions in ½ cup butter./Mix the beaten eggs, cream, buttermilk, 1 cup melted butter, cornmeal, corn, pepper, onions, and half the cheese mixture./Pour into a well-buttered 9-inch square baking dish./Top with remaining cheese./Bake at 350° for 45 minutes./Cool slightly before cutting.

Mrs. James H. Cannon,
Ladies' Committee

Baked Asparagus

"Once you've tried this, you'll never cook asparagus any other way."

Simply put rinsed asparagus no more than two layers deep in a buttered casserole, dot with butter, sprinkle with salt and pepper, cover tightly with aluminum foil and bake at 300° for 30 minutes./Pour over pan juices.

Eve Skinner, Gallery Instructor

- **A good topping for cauliflower is a can of condensed cheddar cheese soup heated with ¼ cup milk.**

Green Pepper Caponatina

"Low-calorie side dish, or part of antipasto first course. Easy and quick to make. Nice with low-calorie lunch of cottage cheese."

3 large green peppers (about 1 pound)
2 medium onions, thinly sliced
   (about 10 ounces)
3 medium tomatoes, peeled and diced
½ teaspoon salt
¼ teaspoon pepper
¼ cup (scant) red wine vinegar

Wash and dry peppers, cut into thin slices lengthwise, discarding seeds./Coat inside of large pot with vegetable oil, heat over low heat, add peppers, onions, tomatoes, salt, and pepper./Cover and cook over low heat for 15 minutes./Uncover and cook 30 minutes longer, stirring often./Stir in vinegar and cook 10 minutes more./Put in covered containers and refrigerate for 2 days before using. (Keeps in refrigerator about 20 days.)

Mrs. John A. Pooley,
Ladies' Committee

Zucchini Favorite

"Just 5 minutes to make this delicious dish."

Serves 6

2 or 3 medium zucchini, sliced
½ teaspoon dill weed
¼-½ cup sour cream

Bring ½ inch water to rapid boil in a large frying pan./Drop in zucchini./Boil for 3 or 4 minutes, stirring so that each slice rests for a minute or two on bottom of pan./Drain thoroughly./Sprinkle dill weed to taste./Fold in sour cream./Serve immediately.

Mrs. Henderson Inches, Jr.,
Ladies' Committee Associate

Green Beans Gretel

"From an Atlanta friend, beans with a unique flavor."

Serves 8

2 pounds green beans
2 tablespoons onion, chopped
2 tablespoons butter
2 tablespoons sugar (or less)
2 tablespoons vinegar
2 teaspoons cornstarch
1 tablespoon prepared mustard
2 teaspoons prepared horseradish
2 tablespoons pimientos

Cook beans and drain, saving liquid./Sauté onion in butter until limp./Combine ¼ cup bean liquid with sugar, vinegar, and cornstarch./Add this mixture to onions./Return to heat and stir until thickened./Blend in 1 tablespoon prepared mustard, horseradish, and pimiento./Add beans; heat gently until hot. (May be made ahead and reheated.)

Mrs. Frank C. Clapp,
Ladies' Committee Associate

White Bean Casserole

"Can be made ahead and heated in oven."

Serves 4

2 tablespoons olive oil
1 onion, chopped
2 cloves garlic, minced
2 tomatoes, peeled, seeded, and chopped
1 bay leaf
2 cloves
pinch of thyme
2 tablespoons parsley, chopped
salt
2 tablespoons Cognac
1 (20-ounce) can Cannellini beans
scallions, chopped, for garnish

Heat olive oil, sauté onion and garlic briefly, then add everything else except beans, including a little bean liquid./Simmer for 30 minutes, then add drained beans and heat.

To serve cold stir in a little vinegar — to taste — and garnish with chopped scallions, including some green.

Eve Skinner, Gallery Instructor

ARISTIDE MAILLOL (French, 1861-1944)
Woodcut from Virgil's *Georgiques*, 1937–1950 (Paris: Philippe Gonin)
Gift of Mr. and Mrs. Peter A. Wick

Garden-Fresh Salads

Molded Asparagus Salad

"A favorite family salad – like a mousse and delicious with cold or hot meat or chicken."

Serves 10-12

1 can undiluted cream of asparagus soup
1 (3-ounce) package lemon gelatin
1 (8-ounce) package cream cheese
½ cup cold water
½ cup mayonnaise
¾ cup celery, chopped
1 tablespoon onion, grated or chopped
½ cup green pepper, chopped
½ cup pecans, chopped

Heat soup over low heat to boiling point./ Remove from heat; add gelatin and stir until dissolved./Add cheese and stir until melted. (I keep this over very low heat to this point, as cheese dissolves more easily.)/Add water and mayonnaise, beat until blended./Stir in remaining ingredients./Turn into 4-cup mold./Chill until firm.

Mrs. Henry F. Cate, Jr.,
Ladies' Committee Associate

Chicken-Rice Salad

"Simple, delicious, and a wonderful summer luncheon or supper salad."

Serves 6

2½ cups cooked rice
3 cups cooked chicken, cut up
2 cups celery, chopped
1 cup cooked peas
½ cup chutney, chopped
½ teaspoon curry
slivered almonds
¾ cup Italian salad dressing

Mix all together./Serve on bed of lettuce.

Mrs. Allan A. Eaton,
Ladies' Committee Associate

Cucumber Mousse

"From a friend in Switzerland who has to buy the lime gelatin in the U.S."

Serves 4-5

1 package lime gelatin
¾ cup boiling water
¼ cup lemon juice
1 tablespoon onion, grated
1 cup sour cream (or yogurt)
1 cup cucumber, finely chopped and seasoned with salt

Dissolve gelatin in boiling water./Add lemon juice and onion./Chill until nearly set./Add sour cream and cucumber and whir in a food processor or blender until creamy./Pour into a mold and chill.

Mrs. S. Leonard Kent,
Ladies' Committee

Green Pepper Salad

"A make-ahead salad with garden-fresh green peppers."

Serves 6

6 green peppers, seeded
oil
oregano
salt
French dressing

Cut green peppers in wide strips./Cover bottom of large skillet with oil and heat./Add pepper strips./Season with oregano and salt./Cook, stirring frequently, until peppers are tender but still hold their shape and color./ Remove to bowl and, while still warm, marinate in French dressing at least an hour at room temperature. (Red peppers or sliced fresh mushrooms may be added for variety and color.)

Mrs. Marsden P. Earle,
Ladies' Committee

Salad Continental

"Delicious and colorful. The best-quality ingredients are essential."

Serves 4

1 pound boiled potatoes, peeled and sliced
10 ounces cooked string beans, cut bite-size
½ cup cooked chick peas, drained
¾ cup celery, sliced
2 green or Bermuda onions, sliced
2 tomatoes, not too ripe
several basil leaves, minced
1 hard-cooked egg, sliced
6 tablespoons Bertolli olive oil
2 tablespoons wine vinegar
1 teaspoon salt
pepper, freshly ground
1 clove garlic, pressed

In a salad bowl combine potatoes, string beans, chick peas, and celery./Toss lightly with dressing made of olive oil, vinegar, garlic, salt, and pepper (additional olive oil optional)./Garnish with onion rings, tomatoes, and egg slices./Sprinkle with minced basil leaves.

Mrs. Carlos H. Tosi,
Ladies' Committee Associate

Crunchy Pea Salad

"An unusual and delicious salad."

Serves 6

1 (10-ounce) package frozen tiny peas, thawed
1 cup celery, chopped
¼ cup green onion, chopped
1 cup cashews or macadamia nuts, chopped
¼ cup crisp bacon bits
1 cup sour cream
¼ cup Garden Café dressing
½ teaspoon salt

Combine peas, celery, onion, nuts, and bacon./Mix together the sour cream and Garden Café dressing and fold in gently./Serve well chilled on a bed of crisp lettuce.

Garden Café Dressing (1 quart)
¾ tablespoon lemon juice
1 cup red wine vinegar
1¼ tablespoons salt
1 teaspoon pepper (not coarse)
1 tablespoon Worcestershire sauce
1 teaspoon Dijon mustard
1 clove garlic, mashed
1 teaspoon sugar
3 cups corn oil

In blender combine all seasonings for dressing, gradually add the oil, and blend.

Mrs. Henry F. Cate, Jr.,
Ladies' Committee Associate

Philippine Salad

"Yum."

Serves 10-12

1 pound spinach
1 head lettuce
1 cucumber, sliced
½ cup peanuts, chopped
1 package flaked coconut
1 red onion, chopped
4-6 tablespoons fresh basil, minced

Proportions may be varied to suit your taste.

Dressing
½ cup sugar
1 cup oil
½ cup vinegar
¼ teaspoon salt
2 teaspoons Spice Islands salad herbs

Dress just before serving and toss.

Carol Howard, Gallery Instructor

Spinach Salad Ring

"Not the usual sweet molded salad."

Serves 6-8

1 package lemon-flavored gelatin
¾ cup hot water
1 tablespoon vinegar
1 cup mayonnaise
1 package chopped, frozen spinach
⅓ cup celery, finely chopped
⅓ cup onion, finely chopped
1 cup cottage cheese

Dissolve gelatin in hot water./Add vinegar and mayonnaise./When cool, beat./Cook spinach just a few minutes and *drain well.*/Add celery, onion, cottage cheese, and spinach to the cooled gelatin mixture./Put into a 6-cup mold and chill until firm./Serve on lettuce bed or cut into individual wedges.

Mrs. Malcolm L. Trayser,
Ladies' Committee Associate

Tabbouleh

"Great salad accompaniment for charcoal-broiled steak. Make it early in the day and refrigerate."

Serves 8

1 cup coarse bulgur wheat (from gourmet or
　　health food store)
4 tomatoes, peeled, seeded, and chopped
2 cups Italian flat-leaf parsley, minced
1 cup scallions, chopped
½ cup olive oil
½ cup fresh mint leaves, minced
　　(or 1½ tablespoons dried mint leaves)
⅓ cup fresh lemon juice
2 teaspoons salt
¼ teaspoon pepper

Soak bulgur in cold water to cover for an hour./Transfer to sieve lined with a double thickness of dampened cheesecloth, tie ends of the cheesecloth together and squeeze until the bulgur is dry./Toss the bulgur and the remaining ingredients together in a bowl and then transfer the salad to a serving bowl lined with romaine leaves.

Mrs. Malcolm L. Trayser,
Ladies' Committee Associate

Cold Rice Salad

"Great for using leftover rice. Best when garden is full of fresh vegetables. I just concoct as I go along."

Serves 8 or more

2 tablespoons butter
1½ cups long-grain rice
2½ cups chicken stock
Good Seasons Italian salad dressing, made
　　according to package directions

all or some of these vegetables:
tomatoes, peeled and chopped
artichokes, marinated and chopped
green or black olives, sliced
onion, chopped
green pepper, sliced
celery pieces, sliced
raw cauliflower, cut in flowerettes
raw broccoli, cut in flowerettes
salt and pepper
parsley, chopped
basil, oregano, tarragon, or mint to taste

In a heavy 1-quart saucepan or skillet, melt the butter and add the rice./Cook over low flame for about 2 minutes, stirring, until rice grains become milky white or opaque./Add the stock, cover, and bring to a boil./Then reduce heat to simmer and cook until all the liquid is absorbed, about 15-20 minutes./Cool the rice, add all or some of the vegetables and herbs and enough salad dressing to moisten.

Mrs. Malcolm L. Trayser,
Ladies' Committee Associate

Cold Curried Rice Salad

"This is a summer salad that can be prepared ahead and is delicious with cold meats or as a separate salad course."

Serves 4

2 cups chilled cooked rice
1 green pepper, shredded
2 tablespoons drained pimientos, cut in short strips
3 tablespoons raisins
2 tablespoons fresh parsley or chervil, chopped
2 tablespoons green onions, chopped (including tops)
½ cup good olive oil
⅓ cup wine vinegar
1 tablespoon lemon juice
1 clove garlic, minced
1 tablespoon sugar
½ teaspoon curry powder
salt and pepper

Using two forks, toss together the rice, green pepper, pimientos, raisins, parsley, and onion./Chill for at least 3 hours./Combine oil, vinegar, lemon juice, garlic, sugar, curry powder, salt, and pepper./Just before serving, pour over salad and toss thoroughly.

This can be served two ways:

1) As an accompaniment for meat, such as cold chicken, it can be arranged in a bowl or casserole and garnished with salad greens, tomato wedges, or green pepper rings.

2) As a first course or salad course, it can be used to stuff tomatoes that have been scooped out, salted, peppered, chilled, and arranged on a bed of greens on individual salad plates.

Anne L. Poulet,
Curator, European Decorative Arts

• **"Four persons are wanted to make a good salad: a spendthrift for oil, a miser for vinegar, a counsellor for salt, and a madman to stir all up."**

Tuna and Macaroni Salad

"This recipe came from my brother Charlie, a very fine cook, who I never expected would put his approval on such an ordinary food as tuna. The first bite of this salad will convert even the most skeptical epicure."

Serves 4-6

1 cup elbow macaroni
1 egg yolk
2 teaspoons imported mustard (similar to Grey Poupon Dijon)
1 teaspoon wine vinegar
½ teaspoon Worcestershire sauce
dash of Tabasco
salt and pepper, freshly ground
1 cup olive oil
2 (7-ounce) cans tuna, packed in oil, preferably imported
½ cup sweet green or red pepper, cubed
½ cup onion, finely chopped
2 tablespoons parsley, finely chopped
tomato wedges for garnish
hard-cooked eggs, quartered, for garnish

Drop the macaroni into a large kettle of boiling salted water./Stir frequently./Boil about 7 minutes or until barely tender./Do not overcook./Drain well./Run cold water over the macaroni and drain thoroughly./Put the egg yolk into a medium-sized mixing bowl./Add the mustard, vinegar, Worcestershire, Tabasco, and salt and pepper to taste./Beat rapidly with a wire whisk (or electric mixer or food processor); gradually add the oil, very slowly at first./When the mayonnaise has thickened, taste it and correct the seasoning if needed./Put the macaroni into a mixing bowl./Drain the tuna and break it into 1-inch pieces./Add it to the bowl./Add the pepper, onion, and parsley, and mix gently./Add the mayonnaise and fold to blend./Spoon the salad onto a round serving dish./Garnish with tomato and egg wedges.

Mrs. Richard M. Fraser,
Ladies' Committee

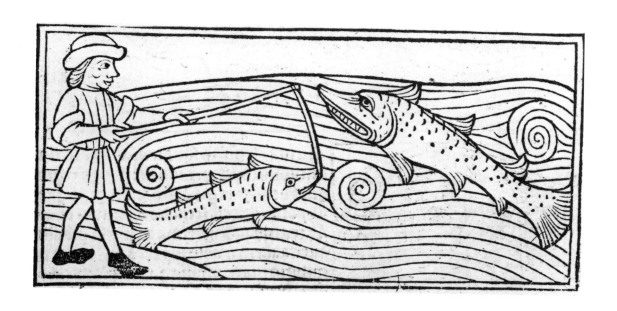

MAYNUS DE MAYNERIIS
Woodcut from *Dialogus Creaturarum Moralisatus,*
1500 (Geneva: Jean Belot)
William F. Warden Fund

Marinated Salad

"This can be made early in the day. It has always been a hit when I've served it."

Serves 4-6

1 cup fresh mushrooms, sliced
1 can hearts of palm
½ cup cherry tomatoes
½ can artichoke hearts (plain), cut into
    fourths
greens (Boston lettuce)
Dressing
1 teaspoon salt
½ teaspoon white pepper
½ teaspoon black pepper
¼ teaspoon dry mustard
1 tablespoon Worcestershire sauce
2 teaspoons lemon juice
1 tablespoon tarragon vinegar
½ teaspoon garlic salt
2 tablespoons French olive oil
6 tablespoons salad oil
1 egg, beaten

Mix all dressing ingredients together./Pour over all salad ingredients except the greens./ Marinate all day./Serve on a bed of lettuce.

Mrs. William F. Sick,
Ladies' Committee

Peachy Jellied Salad

"A pretty two-layer jellied salad for a ladies' luncheon."

Serves 10

1 (16-ounce) can sliced peaches, drained
2 tablespoons apricot brandy
2 packages orange gelatin
2 cups boiling water
1½ cups cold water
½ cup sour cream

Sprinkle peaches with brandy and set aside./ Dissolve gelatin in boiling water./Stir in cold water and chill until thickened./Fold peaches into half the gelatin and spoon into a 6-cup mold./Chill until set, but not firm—about 10 minutes./Blend sour cream into remaining gelatin and spoon over clear layer in mold./ Chill until firm (about 4 hours)./Unmold and garnish with greens.

Mrs. E. Blair Hawley,
Ladies' Committee

Tofu Salad

"A good non-cholesterol substitute for egg salad."

Serves 6-8

2 pounds tofu, mashed (cottage cheese
    texture)
½ cup mayonnaise
2 tablespoons Dijon mustard
1 teaspoon soy sauce
½ teaspoon salt
½ teaspoon garlic, minced (or use garlic
    salt)
1 tablespoon onion, minced
¼ teaspoon turmeric
¼ teaspoon paprika
1 teaspoon celery seed
2 stalks celery, minced
½ cup scallions, minced

Combine all ingredients, mix well, and refrigerate an hour or so for flavors to blend.

Mrs. John H. Halford, Jr.,
Ladies' Committee Associate

• Arrange overlapping slices of tomato aspic; pile marinated artichokes in the center. Beat a bit of the brine from the artichokes into mayonnaise and add a squeeze of lemon for dressing.

ANONYMOUS AMERICAN, 19th century
Egg Salad. Oil painting
M. and M. Karolik Collection

Zesty Molded Salad

"This came to me from an abstract painter who likes red...the rest of us liked the salad!"

Serves 4-6

1 package raspberry gelatin
2 cups V-8 juice
1 tablespoon fresh horseradish
1 tablespoon fresh lemon juice

Heat V-8 juice, add raspberry gelatin, and stir until dissolved./Add horseradish and lemon juice./Pour into mold and refrigerate until jelled./Serve on lettuce with "sweet-sour dressing" in Volume 1.

Mrs. George Marks,
Ladies' Committee Associate

Cinnamon-Applesauce Molded Salad

"This is an old family recipe...a wonderful salad for a buffet...colorful, easy, and delicious. It also doubles or triples very nicely for a large mold."

Serves 6-8

1 package lemon gelatin
¼ cup cinnamon candies (sometimes called "red hots")
1 cup boiling water
1 (15-ounce) jar applesauce

Dissolve gelatin and candies in boiling water./Add applesauce, stir thoroughly, and pour into individual salad molds, or into a 1-quart mold./Refrigerate until firm.

Mrs. C. Roland Christensen,
Ladies' Committee Associate

• **Make a delicious molded cranberry salad by folding cranberry-orange relish into raspberry gelatin made with 3 parts water and 1 part port.**

Mustard Mousse

"Very good with ham."

Serves 4-6

1 envelope plain gelatin
2 tablespoons cold water
2 tablespoons white wine
1 pint sour cream
⅓ cup horseradish
¼ cup chives, chopped
¼ cup Dijon mustard
1 tablespoon hot dry mustard
1 tablespoon lemon juice
dash of Tabasco

Soften gelatin in the water and wine./Place over hot water to dissolve./Stir in the remaining ingredients and pour into a 1-quart mold./Chill, unmold, and serve.

Mrs. Allan R. Finlay,
Ladies' Committee Associate

Mousse Gazpacho

"Make this 24 hours ahead and unmold at serving time."

Serves 8

2 envelopes unflavored gelatin
2 cups V-8 juice
½ onion
1 clove garlic
1 cucumber, seeded
1 small green pepper
salt and pepper
⅓ cup mayonnaise

Sprinkle gelatin over juice./Heat until gelatin is dissolved./Pour into blender with cut-up vegetables./Blend until smooth./Stir in salt, pepper, and mayonnaise./Pour into mold./Chill.

Doris Powell,
Secretary to the Ladies' Committee

LUCAS CRANACH (German, 1472–1553)
Detail of the grape arbor in *St. James.* Woodcut
Harvey D. Parker Collection

ANONYMOUS AMERICAN, 19th century
Tomatoes, Fruit, and Flowers. Oil painting
M. and M. Karolik Collection

24-Hour Salad

"This sounds a bit strange, but I have had so many requests for the recipe I finally had several dozen copies made. I have tripled this, using a punch bowl as the serving dish. Let your food processor do the work."

Serves 10

1 large head iceberg lettuce, shredded
¼ cup onion, thinly sliced
¼ cup celery, diced
1 (6-ounce) can water chestnuts, sliced
¾ pound bacon, fried crisply and crumbled
1 package frozen tiny green peas
2 cups mayonnaise
1 tablespoon granulated sugar
2-3 tablespoons Parmesan cheese, freshly grated

Put the shredded lettuce in the bottom of a deep bowl./On top of the lettuce layer the onion, celery, and water chestnuts./Sprinkle the bacon over them, then break up a box of frozen peas on top of the bacon (the peas should still be frozen)./Spread the mayonnaise on top as if icing a cake top./Be sure to cover the entire area because the mayonnaise forms a seal./Sprinkle sugar over the mayonnaise and cover with a thin layer of Parmesan cheese./Cover with plastic wrap and chill for 24 hours before serving./Mix well.

Mrs. Clarence A. Kemper,
Ladies' Committee

▪ **Drizzle olive oil on sliced, fresh tomatoes; sprinkle with salt and lots of chopped fresh basil.**

Tomato Aspic

"This recipe has the advantage of being absurdly easy to make and of having practically NO calories!"

Serves 4-6

2 cups tomato juice
1 tablespoon dried basil
1 envelope unflavored gelatin
½ cup orange juice (or ¼ cup lemon juice)

To tomato juice add basil and heat to boiling, simmer for 5 minutes./In a measuring cup, soften gelatin in orange juice./Add a small amount of the hot tomato juice and stir, then pour contents of measuring cup back into pot of tomato juice./Stir to dissolve the gelatin completely./Strain into a mold or individual-sized serving containers (plastic containers with lids are great)./Cover and refrigerate until set./Unmold onto lettuce or other greens and serve with cottage cheese./If you like texture, finely chop 1 stalk of celery, 1 very small onion, and one quarter green pepper./When aspic reaches the consistency of an egg white, stir in.

Martha Clough,
Appointments Secretary, Public Education

▪ **For a hearts-of-palm salad, cut canned palm pieces in half lengthwise. Drizzle them with wine vinegar and olive oil, sprinkle with freshly ground pepper, lay slivers of pimiento across the top, and refrigerate several hours before serving.**

▪ **Scoop seeds from fresh tomatoes; invert to drain. Fill with grated cucumber drizzled with French dressing and sprinkled with dill.**

ARISTIDE MAILLOL (French, 1861-1944)
Woodcut from Virgil's *Georgiques,* 1937 – 1950 (Paris: Philippe Gonin)
Gift of Mr. and Mrs. Peter A. Wick

Pasta, Grains & Rice

Pasta in a Pot

"This casserole can be prepared a day or two in advance and refrigerated. Tasty and economical."

Serves 10 generously

2 pounds ground beef
2 medium onions, chopped
1 clove garlic, minced
1 (14-ounce) jar spaghetti sauce
1 (1-pound) can stewed tomatoes
1 (12-ounce) box mushrooms, sliced and sautéed
8 ounces thin spaghetti, cooked
1½ pints sour cream
½ pound provolone cheese, sliced
½ pound mozzarella cheese, sliced

Cook beef and drain excess fat./Add onions, garlic, spaghetti sauce, and stewed tomatoes./Pour half of beef-tomato combination into a large greased casserole dish./Cover with half of mixture of spaghetti and cooked mushrooms./Top with half the amount of sour cream and slices of provolone cheese and mozzarella cheese./Repeat this layered arrangement, ending with mozzarella./Cover and bake at 350° for 35-40 minutes./Uncover until cheese is brown./If casserole has been refrigerated, allow about 10 minutes more.

Mrs. Robert A. Lawrence,
Ladies' Committee Associate

Fettucine Alfredo

"When the original Alfredo in Rome made this dish, he tossed the noodles with a golden spoon and fork. Whatever you use for tossing, this is a great noodle dish."

Serves 4-6

1 pound egg noodles
⅔ cup heavy cream
¼ pound unsalted butter, softened
1 cup Parmesan cheese, grated

Cook the noodles in boiling salted water until tender, but not soft *(al dente)*./Melt half the butter in a heavy saucepan over low heat./Stir in the cream and ¼ cup of the cheese./Add the hot drained noodles and toss gently in the butter mixture, folding as you go, and adding the remaining butter and cheese./Fold, mix, and blend until noodles are coated and creamy./Serve hot with more cheese sprinkled on top if desired.

Mrs. Frederick P. Costanza,
Ladies' Committee Associate

Noodle Pudding

"My mother-in-law's recipe, shared by the whole family."

Serves 12

1 (12-ounce) package egg noodles
4 eggs
6 tablespoons sugar
1 tablespoon salt
½ cup butter, melted
½ pound cottage cheese
6 tablespoons sour cream
½ cup milk

Cook noodles according to package directions./Beat together eggs, sugar, and salt./Add remaining ingredients./Mix with noodles./Bake in well-greased Pyrex dish at 400° for 1 hour or until crusty around dish but not too dry.

Mrs. Benjamin Castleman,
Ladies' Committee Associate

• **If you are in doubt as to how much pasta to cook, keep in mind that 8 ounces of spaghetti swell to about 5 cups cooked; 8 ounces of egg noodles swell to about 4 cups cooked; 8 ounces of macaroni swell to about 4½ cups cooked.**

Shrimp with Vegetables and Pasta

"One of our favorite pasta dishes."

Serves 6-8

3 sticks butter
2½ pounds very large raw shrimp
    (about 10 per pound), shelled and deveined
1½ cups onions, chopped
1 cup scallions, chopped
½ pound mushrooms, sliced
1½ cups chicken stock
½ cup water
¼ pound pasta shells
2 cups canned tomatoes and their juice
salt and pepper
½ cup Parmesan cheese, freshly grated

Melt 1½ sticks butter in large saucepan (at least 3 quart), add shrimp, and sauté over moderately high heat until they turn pink./Stir in onions, scallions, and mushrooms, sautéeing until vegetables are soft (about 6 minutes)./ Remove the shrimp to a separate dish and keep them warm./Add to the pan chicken stock and water and bring to a boil./Stir in pasta shells and cook the mixture for approximately 15 minutes, stirring occasionally./Stir in tomatoes, salt, and pepper, simmering for 5 minutes (up to this point, cooking could be done ahead)./Return shrimp to pan and heat./Taste again for seasoning./Pour in 1½ sticks of butter, which has been melted and heated until it is deep golden./Sprinkle with Parmesan cheese./Serve with a green salad and French bread.

Mrs. John J. McArdle, Jr.,
Ladies' Committee

Pastiera

"This noodle ring is delicious hot or cold. Serve as a meat accompaniment or cut into squares after it is "set" and serve as an hors d'oeuvre."

Serves 6

2 cups uncooked noodles
4 eggs, well beaten
1 cup milk
½ cup butter, melted
½ cup yellow cheese, grated
½ tablespoon onion, grated
2 tablespoons parsley, chopped
½ teaspoon salt

Cook noodles according to package directions and rinse with cold water./Add remaining ingredients and pour into well-buttered ring baking dish./Set in pan of hot water and bake, covered with foil, at 350° for 45 minutes.

The Italians sometimes make this richer by adding ½ pound of ricotta cheese to the mixture before baking.

Mrs. Frederick P. Costanza,
Ladies' Committee Associate

Gnocchi

"A different version of gnocchi, deliciously good."

Serves 8-10

2 cups hot milk
1 cup hot water
¾ cup farina
1 teaspoon salt
½ teaspoon dry mustard
1½ cups sharp cheddar cheese, grated
3 eggs, well beaten
1 cup heavy cream

Cook the first 5 ingredients in top of double boiler until thick (about 10 minutes or more)./ Add 1 cup of cheese./When melted, stir in the eggs./Spread in shallow baking dish and let stand several hours or overnight./When ready to bake cover with remaining grated cheese and cream./Bake at 350° 40-45 minutes or until light brown and bubbly./Serve at once.

Mrs. James Lawrence,
Ladies' Committee Associate

Rice with Peas and Vegetable Sauté

"Spanish-derived in that certain key components are those of a paella; Oriental in its method and seasonings."

Serves 4-6

1 cup raw brown rice
2 teaspoons dried tarragon
2 cups water
½ cup dried split green peas
12-inch strip wakame
 (or other sea vegetable)
2 cups water
½ cup onion, chopped
3 tablespoons butter

Cook rice with tarragon in salted water for 40 minutes; cook peas for an hour with wakame./ Cut wakame into small pieces; combine with peas and rice and toss lightly with onion sautéed in butter; set aside in warm oven while preparing the following:

2 cups cauliflower, chopped
2 tablespoons butter
1 cup mushrooms, sliced
8 scallions, chopped
1 cup fresh peas
1 teaspoon salt
1 teaspoon fresh tarragon (or ½ teaspoon
 dried), chopped fine
1 tablespoon fresh parsley, chopped
½ teaspoon fresh ginger root, grated
½ cup slivered almonds
1 tablespoon lemon juice
1 tablespoon Tamari

Steam cauliflower pieces briefly in a little water in the bottom of a skillet./When pieces

are tender and water has evaporated, remove cauliflower and stir-fry mushrooms and scallions in butter. Add fresh peas, herbs, and almonds and cook 2 minutes./Return cauliflower to skillet and reheat, adding lemon juice and Tamari last./Surround with rice and peas on serving platter; garnish with parsley and slices of radish.

Judy Spear, Editor, Publications

Mediterranean Pilaf

"So easy and so delicious."

Serves 8

1½ cups uncooked rice
4 tablespoons vegetable oil
½ cup golden raisins
½ teaspoon turmeric
½ teaspoon curry powder
½ tablespoon soy sauce
3 cups chicken broth

Mix rice, oil, raisins, turmeric, curry, and soy sauce./Cover with hot chicken broth./Simmer at low heat 20 minutes or until liquid is absorbed.

Carol Howard, Gallery Instructor

Peanut Rice

"Good with chicken...Indonesian flavor."

Serves 10-12

7 cups cooked rice
1 cup roasted peanuts, coarsely chopped
½ cup butter, melted
½ cup honey
1 teaspoon ginger
2 teaspoons cinnamon
parsley to garnish

Combine all ingredients except parsley./Cook a few minutes and keep warm until ready to serve./Sprinkle with parsley.

Carol Howard, Gallery Instructor

California Rice

*"A recipe from my mother-in-law, who served
this often. Nice change as a meat accompaniment."*

Serves 8

3 tablespoons butter
4 tablespoons flour
2 cups milk
2 cups cooked rice (1 cup raw)
½ teaspoon salt
¼ teaspoon paprika
⅓ cup onion, chopped
½ cup cheddar cheese, shredded
½ cup pimiento-stuffed olives, chopped
½ cup bread crumbs
2 tablespoons butter, melted

Melt 3 tablespoons butter; add flour./When
blended, add milk and cook until creamy./Stir
constantly, adding rice, salt, paprika, onion,
olives, and cheese./Mix and pour into buttered shallow baking dish./Cover with crumbs
that have been mixed with 2 tablespoons
melted butter./Bake at 350° for 30 minutes.
(Will keep in warm oven.)

*Mrs. Mayo A. Shattuck,
Ladies' Committee Associate*

Risotto

"Simple, elegant."

Serves 4

1 medium onion, finely chopped
½ cup butter
2 cups long-grain rice
½ cup dry white wine
4 cups chicken broth
¼ teaspoon saffron
generous sprinkle of parsley
Parmesan cheese, freshly grated
salt and pepper

Sauté onion in butter until translucent./Stir in
rice./Add wine and chicken broth./Cover and
bring to a boil, then reduce to simmer and cook
until rice is tender (about 20 minutes)./Add
saffron, parsley, Parmesan cheese to taste, and
salt and pepper if needed.

Variation: My Mediterranean family members
send to Italy by air freight for mushrooms./
Fresh, local mushrooms will do./The general
rule is that the more ugly the mushroom the
more flavorful it may be.

*Maurice ("Peter") Tonissi II, Esq.,
Receptionist, Members' Room*

Tian de Courgettes au Riz

*"In Provence, this is cooked in an earthenware
dish called a 'tian,' which has given its name
to the mixture of vegetables cooked in it."*

Serves 6-8

2 medium onions, minced
2 cloves garlic, minced
3-4 tablespoons olive oil
2 pounds zucchini, unpeeled, grated
½ cup raw rice, cooked 10 minutes in boil-
    ing water
salt and pepper
2 eggs
⅔ cup cheddar cheese, grated
¼ cup Parmesan cheese, grated

Sauté onions and garlic in olive oil./Add
zucchini./Cook together for 8-10 minutes./
Add rice to zucchini mixture./Add salt and
pepper./Add eggs and cheese, reserving
enough cheese for topping./Pour into a shallow baking dish coated with olive oil./Drizzle
a little olive oil on top./Sprinkle with remaining cheese./Bake at 375° until top is well
browned (about 35 minutes).

*Doris Powell,
Secretary to the Ladies' Committee*

Iulius, Augustus, nec non et Iunius Aestas.   AESTAS   Frugiferas aruis fert Aestas torrida meßeis.
Adoles   tentir imago

PIETER BRUEGHEL (Netherlandish, ca. 1525–1569)
Summer from "The Four Seasons." Engraving
Seth K. Sweetser Fund

Four-Corners Polenta

"Several years ago we broke our journey at mid-day not because we felt the need of another cathedral set in a medieval square, or a market or a festival that might have local costumes and a hurdy gurdy. No indeed. None of these existed where we stopped (not from choice, but because a rear tire had experienced its last good year and our spare was not up to a jour-ney of any sizable kilometric length). Our stop-ping place was on one fourth of the "village" area, namely on one of its four corners and specifically the corner wholly occupied by a most welcome gasoline station. On the oppo-site side of the intersection remained the cellar and partial walls of what once was a dwelling, perhaps a farmhouse because to the rear of the corners farmland stretched to the horizon. A pottery (for want of another name) shop spewed its garish goods all over the third cor-ner across the highway with a green pottery Teddy Bear being the special of the day. The station attendant told us the restaurant on the fourth corner was "verra, verra good." We wasted no time taking his word for it. And good it was! More than that, it was superb. In all northern Italy we never ate a polenta to equal theirs. While a most willing, coopera-tive, and able mechanic repaired our tires, we dined in simple but lovely surroundings with food that could challenge any city, town, vil-lage, or four corners restaurant.

Serves 6-8

1 cup stone-ground corn meal
5 cups cold water
1 teaspoon salt
1½ cups very sharp cheese, grated
1 small jar pimientos, chopped
½ teaspoon pepper, freshly ground
1 teaspoon oregano leaves
½ cup Parmesan cheese, grated
1 tablespoon butter

Place corn meal in top of double boiler./ Gradually add 1 cup cold water and salt and stir until blended./Cook over direct heat, stir-ring constantly until the meal is well blended./Remove from direct heat and place over boiling water in the double boiler./Add gradually 4 cups of cold water./Stir constantly until mixture is well blended and begins to thicken./Reduce heat and simmer gently, stir-ring occasionally, for 30 minutes./Add grated sharp cheese, pimientos, pepper, and oregano./Cook until cheese is melted./Butter a deep casserole or soufflé dish and pour the mixture into the dish./Top with grated Parme-san cheese and dot with butter./Bake at 375° about 25 minutes or until golden brown.

Clementine Brown,
Manager, Public Information
(with thanks to Libby Alsberg
of Marblehead)

Pesto Genovese

"One of the most popular of all pasta dishes."

Serves 4-6

1½ cups fresh basil leaves
½ cup olive oil
½ cup Parmesan cheese
½ cup pine nuts (pignoli) or walnuts (pine nuts are better flavored)
⅓ cup flat-leaf parsley
½ teaspoon salt
2 garlic cloves, minced
⅛ pound butter

Wash, strip leaves from stems of basil and pack down firmly to measure./Gradually mix all ingredients in blender or food processor until smooth (mixture will be rather thick)./Serve at room temperature over cooked thin spaghetti or linguini./This pesto may be frozen for use as above, or as seasoning in various dishes./ Freeze in small muffin tins, then transfer into baggies for storage./You can then enjoy pesto at any time of year!

Mrs. Frederick P. Costanza,
Ladies' Committee Associate

KITAGAWA UTAMARO (Japanese, 1753 – 1806)
The Popular Waitress Okita. Woodblock print. Spaulding Collection

Operatic Rice

*"I serve this to a touring opera company includ-
ing leading artists, "grips," and truck drivers.
A smash hit every time!"*

Serves 8-10

**1 cup wild rice, or combination wild and
  white, cooked according to package directions
1 pound mushrooms, cleaned and quartered
1 package frozen baby lima beans
½ stick butter
½ cup light cream, more or less
salt and pepper**

Sauté the mushrooms in butter until they
exude their juices./Reserve with juices./
Prepare beans according to package instructions.

When rice, mushrooms, and beans have been
cooked, combine and mix well in the casserole, adding cream slowly while stirring and
fluffing./Taste for seasoning, which should be
quite delicate./Finished consistency should
be moist but not wet./When cool, if not to be
used at once, cover and refrigerate./It reheats
nicely, but may need a bit more liquid./If you
feel it has enough cream, moisten with chicken
broth./This can stand alone, with green salad
and French bread, or with cold meats, fowl, etc.

*Mrs. Richard H. Thompson,
Ladies' Committee Associate*

Millet-Lentil Curry

*"A happy combination of vegetables, grains,
and spices borrowed from the Indian and
Chinese traditions."*

Serves 6

**½ cup millet, toasted lightly in skillet
½ cup red lentils
2½ cups water**

Boil together on medium-low heat for 15 minutes, until water has evaporated. While cooking, prepare the following:

**2 cups cabbage, coarsely cut
2 stalks celery, chopped
2 medium onions, chopped
1 cup carrots, diced
1 clove garlic
1 teaspoon salt
1-2 teaspoons curry powder
½ teaspoon ginger root, ground
1 cup cooked garbanzos
1 cup tofu, mashed
2-4 teaspoons lemon juice
1-2 tablespoons Tamari**

Sauté vegetables and spices; add tofu and
garbanzos./Layer with millet-lentil mixture in
casserole and refrigerate until ready to serve
(allowing flavors to blend). Moisten with
lemon juice and Tamari and heat at 350° for
30 minutes.

Judy Spear, Editor, Publications

Wild Rice Casserole

"This excellent recipe from a Minnesota cousin may be made ahead, frozen, and reheated.

Serves 8-10

1 cup wild rice (or ½ cup wild rice and ½ cup brown rice)
½ pound fresh mushrooms, sliced
½ cup butter or margarine
3 tablespoons onion or scallions, chopped
3 cups chicken broth
½ cup sliced water chestnuts or slivered almonds

Wash wild rice thoroughly./Lightly brown rice in butter with mushrooms, onion, and water chestnuts./Add the broth./Turn into a 1½ or 2-quart casserole, cover, and bake at 325° until the rice is tender (about 1-1½ hours).

Mrs. Norris H. Hoyt,
Ladies' Committee Associate

Rice and Mushroom Ring

"Delicious with a meat or chicken dinner or as a main luncheon dish with creamed chicken."

Serves 8

1 cup rice
1 pound mushrooms, chopped
2 tablespoons butter
salt

Cook rice and rinse in cold water./Sauté mushrooms in butter./Add rice and salt, and simmer 15 minutes./Put mixture in buttered ring mold; set in pan of boiling water and bake at 350° about 45 minutes.

Serve with buttered peas or any creamed entrée in center.

Esther Rome, Gallery Instructor

ARISTIDE MAILLOL (French, 1861-1944)
Woodcut from Virgil's *Georgiques*, 1937–1950 (Paris: Philippe Gonin)
Gift of Mr. and Mrs. Peter A. Wick

ISAAK SOREAU (Flemish, 1604 – ?)
Still Life with Grapes and Other Fruit. Oil painting
Juliana Cheney Edwards Collection

Desserts

Ice Cream Cake

"A colorful, delicious do-ahead dessert."

Serves 8-10

2 packages lady fingers
1 quart mint chocolate chip ice cream
1 pint raspberry ice or sherbet
1 quart coffee ice cream
¼ pound butter
2 (4-ounce) packages German sweet
   chocolate
2 (1-ounce) squares semisweet chocolate
4 eggs, beaten

Line a 9-inch springform pan, sides and bottom, with lady fingers./Chill.

Soften mint ice cream and spread smoothly on bottom lady fingers./Cover with foil and freeze completely./Soften raspberry ice and repeat the procedure./Soften coffee ice cream and repeat.

Melt butter and chocolates over low heat./Add eggs all at once to mixture and beat until shiny./Cool completely and pour over coffee ice cream./Cover with foil and freeze.

Mrs. John A. Kirkpatrick, Jr.,
Ladies' Committee

Dutch-Apple Cake

"A yummy apple recipe. My family likes it much better than 'Brown Betty'."

Serves 8

1¼ cups sifted flour
1 teaspoon baking powder
1 tablespoon sugar
½ cup butter
1 egg, slightly beaten
½ teaspoon vanilla
3 medium (cooking) apples
¾ cup sugar
1¼ tablespoons flour
salt
2 tablespoons butter
½ teaspoon cinnamon

Sift flour, measure, and sift with baking powder and sugar./Cut in butter until mixture is crumbly./Add vanilla to egg and blend with flour mixture./Press evenly onto bottom and sides of 8-inch square pan./Arrange peeled, sliced apples in overlapping layers to cover dough./Combine remaining ingredients and sprinkle over apples./Bake at 350° for 45 minutes or until apples are tender and topping is golden brown./Cut into squares and serve warm or cold with whipped cream or a scoop of vanilla ice cream.

Mrs. George W. Ferguson
Ladies' Committee

Strawberries Fondant

"Elegant, quick dessert."

Serves 6 or more

2 pints strawberries
1 tablespoon instant coffee powder
   or granules
1½ tablespoons boiling water
2 tablespoons butter, softened
1 egg yolk
1¾ cups powdered sugar, sifted

Wash berries; dry thoroughly./In small bowl dissolve instant coffee in boiling water./Add remaining ingredients./Beat until thick and smooth./Dip tips of berries in mixture./Arrange on plate (a pink Staffordshire is my favorite), stem end down./Chill until set, about 30 minutes. (Can be made early in the day.)

Mrs. William A. Slade,
Ladies' Committee Associate

• Layer crushed macaroons with fresh or frozen raspberries, sprinkle generously with Framboise, and drown in thick, cold custard.

Bottomless Cranberry Pie

"Good warm or cold."

Serves 6

2 cups cranberries
⅓ to ½ cup sugar
½ cup nuts, coarsely chopped

Thoroughly grease a deep 10-inch pie pan, spread cranberries evenly over bottom, sprinkle with sugar and nuts./Cover with:

2 eggs, well beaten
1 cup sugar
1 cup butter or margarine, melted
¼ cup vegetable oil
1 cup flour

Beat eggs well; gradually add sugar, continuing to beat./Add shortening and oil and stir in flour./Spread over cranberries./Bake 1 hour at 325° until crust is golden brown./Serve in wedges, topped with vanilla ice cream or almond-flavored whipped cream.

Mrs. John H. Halford, Jr.,
Ladies' Committee Associate

Aunt Barbara's Strawberry Cheese Pie

"Aunt Barbara was a marvelous cook!"

Serves 10

Graham Cracker Crust
2 cups graham cracker crumbs
½ cup butter or margarine, melted
½ cup sugar
¼ teaspoon cinnamon

Mix well./Press into 10-inch pie plate with fingers or back of spoon./Bake 8 minutes at 375°.

Filling
1 pound cream cheese
¾ cup sugar
2 eggs
½ teaspoon vanilla
¼ teaspoon cinnamon

Allow cheese to come to room temperature./Beat until smooth./Add sugar, eggs, vanilla, and cinnamon./Mix well./Place in pie shell./Bake 20 minutes at 325°./Remove from oven./Raise heat to 450°.

Topping
½ pint sour cream
2 tablespoons sugar
½ teaspoon vanilla

Mix together./Evenly cover top of pie./Bake 5 minutes at 450° and remove from oven./Cool and refrigerate for 3-4 hours.

Strawberry Glaze
1 large package frozen sliced strawberries, thawed
2 tablespoons cornstarch

Drain juice from thawed berries./Place berries on pie./Cook juice and 2 tablespoons cornstarch until thick and clear./Cover strawberries and chill.

Katherine B. Duane,
Operations Coordinator

Caramel Pudding

"Another old family recipe./A light finish to any meal./The ingredients are most likely always on hand."

Serves 4

1 cup brown sugar
¼ cup water
1 tablespoon gelatin
⅓ cup water
4 egg whites
½ cup walnuts, chopped

Boil the sugar and ¼ cup water until a thread spins or the syrup reaches the soft-ball stage./ Soften the gelatin in ⅓ cup water and add to the syrup, stirring until the gelatin dissolves./ Beat the egg whites until stiff, then add the syrup slowly in a steady stream./Fold in the nuts carefully and transfer to a serving bowl./Refrigerate until firm./Serve with the following:

Custard Sauce
4 egg yolks
½ cup sugar
2 cups milk, scalded
1 tablespoon vanilla

In the top of a double boiler, mix the egg yolks and the sugar well./Slowly add the scalded milk and cook over low heat until sauce thickens, stirring constantly./Add vanilla, strain, and cool.

Mrs. Malcolm L. Trayser,
Ladies' Committee Associate

Apple Pudding with Calvados

"A taste of Normandy."

Serves 4

4-5 cooking apples, peeled, cored, and
  chopped
½ cup water
3 tablespoons sugar
1½ cups soft bread crumbs
2-3 tablespoons Calvados
light brown sugar
butter
crème fraîche **or whipped cream**

Cook apples, sugar, and water until soft./ Cool./Mix with bread crumbs and Calvados./ Put in a buttered baking dish, sprinkle with brown sugar, and dot with butter./Heat in 350° oven until bubbly./Serve with *crème fraîche* or whipped cream.

Mrs. John A. Pooley
Ladies' Committee

Australian Fruit Cake

"Wouldn't be Christmas without it. Best if aged a month."

Yield: 1 (9-inch) round cake

1½ cups raisins
¾ cup currants
½ cup mixed peel
¼ pound blanched almonds
½ cup crystallized cherries
4 tablespoons brandy or whiskey
2 sticks butter
⅔ cup brown sugar
½ cup white sugar
4 eggs
2⅓ cups flour
½ teaspoon allspice
½ teaspoon baking powder
½ teaspoon nutmeg
½ teaspoon salt

Combine fruit and nuts and sprinkle with 2 tablespoons brandy./Set aside until following day.

Line 9-inch round tin with two thicknesses of cooking parchment, extending paper 1 inch above tin.

Cream butter and sugar./Add unbeaten eggs, one at a time, beating mixture well after each one./Add half the fruit and remainder of brandy and stir.

Sift flour, spices, baking powder, and salt and gradually add half to mixture./Add remainder of fruit and then gradually remainder of flour./ Stir well.

Place mixture in prepared tin in middle shelf of 325° oven./Bake about 2 hours (test after 1½ hours)./Turn out of tin to cool.

Mrs. Jennifer Weber,
Ladies' Committee

• **To make superfine sugar, whir regular sugar in a blender.**

Graham-Cracker Cake

"A rich dessert but one even dieters enjoy!"

Serves 10

1 cup sugar
⅓ cup butter
1 cup milk
4 eggs, separated (or 5 whites, 3 yolks)
1 cup walnuts, chopped
23 graham cracker squares, ground
2 tablespoons flour
2 teaspoons baking powder
1 teaspoon vanilla
pinch of salt

Cream butter and sugar./Add milk, beaten egg yolks, nuts, graham crackers, flour, baking powder, vanilla and salt./Fold in beaten egg whites./Bake in 2 well-greased round cake pans at 350° for 20 minutes.

Filling and Frosting
¼ pound sweet butter
1 pound confectioner's sugar
1 egg
2-3 tablespoons strong coffee
1 teaspoon vanilla

Cream butter and sugar, add egg, coffee, and vanilla./Spread between layers and frost top and sides. (Bake cake ahead a day or two; frost the day you plan to serve.)

Mrs. Haskell Cohn,
Ladies' Committee Associate

▪ Cut bananas in half lengthwise. Cook slightly in brown sugar and butter. Pour in Myers Rum and enough heavy cream to mellow the rum.

▪ Make a sour cream dip for strawberries by beating together ½ cup confectioner's sugar, 1 teaspoon lemon juice, 1 teaspoon grated lemon rind, and 1 cup sour cream.

Date-Nut Cake

"Stores well. Makes a nice holiday gift."

Yield: 1 (9-inch) round cake

¾ cup butter or margarine
1¼ cups light brown sugar
4 eggs
1 cup cheddar cheese, shredded
3½ cups sifted all-purpose flour
½ teaspoon baking soda
1 teaspoon salt
¾ cup milk
¼ cup dark rum
2 (8-ounce) packages pitted dates, cut up
2 cups walnuts, chopped

Grease and flour 9 x 3-inch tube pan./Beat butter or margarine and sugar in large bowl until well blended./Add eggs, one at a time, beating with each addition./Beat in cheese./Sift flour, soda, and salt together./Add alternately with milk to butter-sugar mixture./Add rum./Beat until smooth and blended./Stir in dates and walnuts./Pour into prepared pan./Bake at 300° for 2-2½ hours until cake tests done./Cool and remove from pan./Decorate with candied fruit if desired./May be stored several weeks in covered container to mellow flavor./May be baked in loaf pan.

Mrs. George D. Mason,
Ladies' Committee Associate

Pumpkin-Pie Cake

"A favorite holiday recipe, easy to prepare…far simpler than making a pumpkin pie."

Serves 8-10

1 (15-ounce) can pumpkin
1 (13-ounce) can evaporated milk
4 eggs, beaten
4 teaspoons pumpkin pie spice mix
½ teaspoon salt
1 cup sugar (brown or white)
1 box yellow cake mix (dry)
1½ cups nuts, chopped
1½ sticks butter, melted

Mix first 6 ingredients together thoroughly.
Pour into greased and floured 13 x 9-inch pan./
Sprinkle cake mix and nuts on top of pumpkin
mixture./Then drizzle melted butter over all./
Bake at 350° for 35 minutes./
Reduce heat to 325° for about 25 minutes
more, or until the pudding is set in the
middle./This can be served warm or cold with
a topping of whipped cream, ice cream, or
hard sauce.

Mrs. William J. Brown, Jr.,
Ladies' Committee Associate

Vatkattu Karpalo Puuro

"An Americanized version of a favorite Finnish
cranberry whip dessert."

Serves 6-8

2 cups cranberries
4 cups water
½ cup uncooked farina (scant)
1 cup sugar

Boil cranberries in water until skins pop./
Mash and strain cranberries thoroughly./Heat
the cranberry juice to boiling and *sprinkle* in
the farina, stirring to prevent lumps./Add
sugar.

Cook slowly for 20 minutes./Pour into large
bowl, cool slightly, and whip at high speed
until light and fluffy and 2 or 3 times original
volume.

Serve with *light* cream.

Mrs. Savele Syrjala,
Ladies' Committee Associate

• **Serve strawberries with their stems with 2**
sake cups for each guest, one with pow-
dered sugar, one with Cointreau. Dip the
strawberries first in Cointreau, then in
sugar.

Pineapple Crunch

"An imaginative blend of flavors."

Serves 8

1 ripe pineapple, cubed
4 tart green apples (like Granny Smith),
peeled and chopped
1 lime
½ cup pecans, chopped
¾ cup flour
½ cup brown sugar
6 tablespoons butter, softened

Sprinkle pineapple and apples with lime juice
and grated zest from lime./Spread in 9- or 10-
inch pie plate or quiche pan./Mix flour, sugar,
nuts, and butter and spread on top of fruit./
Bake at 350° until bubbling and brown (35-45
minutes).

Mrs. James Cannon,
Ladies' Committee Associate

Rhubarb Mousse

"A tart-sweet dessert."

Serves 10

4 teaspoons gelatin
3 tablespoons cold water
2½ cups cooked rhubarb, sweetened
1 tablespoon lemon juice
3 tablespoons Crème de Cassis
3 egg whites
1 tablespoon sugar
1 cup heavy cream, whipped

Soften gelatin in cold water./Purée rhubarb in
blender or food processor./Heat gelatin to dissolve and stir into rhubarb./Cool, stirring over
ice cubes, then add lemon juice, Cassis, 3 egg
whites whipped with 1 tablespoon sugar until
stiff but not dry./Fold in 1 cup whipped cream./
Freezes nicely./Delicious with a custard
sauce or more Cassis dribbled over the top.

Mrs. James Cannon,
Ladies' Committee Associate

HONORÉ DAUMIER (French, 1808-1879)
A Family Lunch, 1855. Lithograph
Babcock Bequest

Whipped-Cream Cake with Fresh Fruit Sauce

"My mother's recipe."

Serves 10

2 eggs, beaten
1 cup heavy cream
1⅓ cups flour
1 cup sugar
2 teaspoons baking powder
¼ teaspoon salt
⅛ teaspoon mace
½ teaspoon almond extract

Beat cream until frothy; combine with eggs and almond extract./Sift flour, sugar, baking powder, salt, and mace./Carefully fold flour mixture into cream mixture./Pour into greased and floured loaf pan./Bake at 375° for about 40 minutes./Slice and serve with the following:

Sauce
3 cups sweetened peaches, quartered
3 cups sweetened blackberries
2 cups chilled sherry-flavored custard sauce

This cake stands alone very nicely./Or serve it with a dusting of confectioner's sugar, a glass of champagne, and strawberries.

Doris Powell,
Secretary to the Ladies' Committee

Russian Nut Torte

"Every Russian cook has her own recipe. This one is a family favorite."

Serves 12-14

8 eggs, separated
10 tablespoons sugar
½ cup fine bread crumbs
2 cups walnuts, finely chopped
½ cup liqueur or wine
1 teaspoon vanilla

Beat egg yolks with an electric mixer until they are very thick and nearly white./Fold in bread crumbs and nuts./Add liqueur and vanilla./Fold in stiffly beaten whites.Bake in 2 round buttered and floured 9 x 1½-inch pans (or 1 pan double the size) at 350° for 45 minutes./Test at 35 minutes and 40 minutes to be sure not to overbake./Decorate with powdered sugar and serve in wedges.

Mrs. Victor A. Lutnicki,
Ladies' Committee

Orange Mousse

"The sauce makes this mousse special."

Serves 6-8

1 envelope plain gelatin
1¼ cups orange juice
grated peel of a large orange
3 eggs, separated
½ cup sugar
⅓ cup whipping cream

Soak gelatin in ¼ cup orange juice./Heat the rest of the orange juice and the peel and dissolve the softened gelatin in it./Whip egg yolks and sugar until thick and light./Stir into orange juice, and over *very* low heat (or over hot water), cook until slightly thickened (just a few minutes)./Cool to room temperature./Whip egg whites until stiff./Whip cream./Fold both into orange juice mixture./Pour into mold and refrigerate until firm.

Sauce
2 or 3 seedless oranges
½ cup bitter orange marmalade
½ cup Grand Marnier or Cointreau

Remove white membrane from orange sections./Cut into bite-size pieces./Combine with marmalade and liqueur and refrigerate. (Best made the day before to let flavors blend.)

Miss Ellen Stillman,
Ladies' Committee Associate

Prunes in Wine

"Ambrosia!"

Serves 10-12

1 pound pitted prunes
sweet or dry red wine
honey
½ lemon, sliced and seeded
a few whole cloves

Arrange prunes in large skillet in one layer and pour in wine to barely cover./Add honey, according to the sweetness of the wine./ Scatter lemon slices and cloves./Simmer, turning prunes occasionally until you have prunes left in a small amount of luscious, red sticky syrup./Discard cloves./Good plain or with cream.

Mrs. Selwyn Kudisch,
Ladies' Committee

Ginger Mousse

"Delicate ginger flavor for ginger devotées."

Serves 10

3 cups cold milk
2 envelopes gelatin
½ cup sugar, plus 6 tablespoons
1 teaspoon nutmeg
¼ cup crystallized ginger, chopped
1 tablespoon fresh ginger, grated
** (or ½ teaspoon ground)**
4 teaspoons cornstarch
2 tablespoons dark rum
3 eggs, separated
⅔ cup heavy cream

Lightly grease the inside of an 8-cup mold with corn oil./Combine milk, gelatin, and ½ cup of sugar in saucepan./Bring to simmer and stir until gelatin dissolves./Stir in nutmeg, crystallized ginger, and fresh ginger./ Blend cornstarch with rum and add to saucepan, stirring until mixture thickens./

Beat yolks and add rapidly./Remove from heat and cool./Beat egg whites; when almost stiff beat in 4 tablespoons sugar./Beat until stiff./ Fold into mixture./Whip the cream; when almost stiff gradually add remaining 2 tablespoons sugar, beating constantly./Fold into mousse mixture./Pour into mold./Refrigerate overnight.

Mrs. John B. Sears,
Ladies' Committee

Palace White Chocolate Mousse

"Adapted from the mousse served at the Palace Restaurant in New York."

Serves 10-12

1 quart heavy cream, well chilled
1 cup egg whites (8 large)
1 pound sugar cubes
1 cup water
2 pounds white chocolate, cut in small cubes

Whip cream and set aside./Place sugar in saucepan, pour water over cubes./Boil until sugar melts and syrup reaches hard-ball stage (255° on candy thermometer)./Whip egg whites to form soft peaks, then reduce speed of mixer and slowly pour in syrup./Add chocolate pieces to warm mixture./They should melt somewhat./Combine mousse base with cream./Pour in serving bowl and chill at least 4 hours.

Sauce

Purée 3 quarts of strawberries; stir in ¼ cup superfine sugar, ¼ cup Kirsch, and pinch of salt.

Mrs. John B. Sears,
Ladies' Committee

• **Sauté apple slices in brown sugar and butter. Blaze with Calvados. Pass cold custard sauce.**

PAUL CÉZANNE (French, 1839–1906)
Fruit and a Jug. Oil painting
Bequest of John T. Spaulding

Meringue Nut Torte

"Always brings raves!"

Serves 6-8

1½ cups saltines, crumbed very fine
2 cups pecans, chopped
2 teaspoons baking powder
6 egg whites
2 cups sugar
2 teaspoons almond extract
whipped cream

Mix saltine crumbs with pecans and baking powder./Beat egg whites until stiff but not dry; add sugar, a tablespoon at a time, beating after each addition, as for any meringue. Add almond extract./Fold in crumb-nut mixture./ Spread in 2 greased and floured 9-inch cake pans that have removable slip bottoms (mixture should be slightly rounded in the center)./Bake at 325° for 40 minutes./Remove from pans./Cool on a rack./Put the 2 layers together with sweetened and flavored whipped cream and garnish with strawberries.

Mrs. George D. Mason,
Ladies' Committee Associate

Pumpkin Flan

"My mother's recipe. A surprising change from the standard flan."

Serves 9-12

¾ cup sugar
½ cup water
1 (15-ounce) can pumpkin pie filling
¾ cup sugar
½ teaspoon salt
1 teaspoon cinnamon
⅓ cup water
1 (13-ounce) can evaporated milk
1½ teaspoons vanilla

Heat ¾ cup sugar and ½ cup water in a heavy saucepan until the sugar caramelizes and turns dark brown./Remove from heat immediately and pour into 1½-quart oven-proof mold./ Swirl the mold with one hand while you pour with the other so that the sides of the mold as well as the bottom are coated./This must be done quickly or the caramel will solidify.

In a large bowl combine pumpkin pie filling, ¾ cup sugar, salt, cinnamon, and eggs and mix well./Stir in the water, milk, and vanilla./Pour the entire mixture into the coated mold./Place the mold in a pan of boiling water and bake at 350° for 1½ hours or until an inserted knife comes out clean./Cool, then refrigerate./ Unmold to serve./The caramel coating will become the sauce for the flan.

Mrs. Malcolm L. Trayser,
Ladies' Committee Associate

Maple-Syrup Mold

"Delicious!"

Serves 8

1 tablespoon unflavored gelatin
½ cup milk
1 cup pure maple syrup
5 egg yolks, beaten
1½ cups heavy cream, whipped

Soak gelatin in milk./Heat maple syrup in the top of a double boiler and add beaten egg yolks./Add the gelatin and beat until thick./ Cool./Fold in whipped cream, reserving a small portion for garnish./Pour into a melon mold and place in refrigerator until firm./ Serve garnished with reserved whipped cream.

Mrs. Frederick N. Blodgett,
Ladies' Committee Associate

Mimi's Trifle

"A very special holiday dessert for our family, which my husband's mother brought back from England over 50 years ago."

Serves 10

sponge cake (can be made ahead from your
   own recipe)
1 jar raspberry jam (homemade if possible)
2 medium-sized bananas, sliced
½ cup English walnuts, chopped
¼ cup orange juice, freshly squeezed
¾ cup cream sherry
crème anglaise (or your own
   boiled custard)
1 cup heavy cream, whipped

Cut sponge cake into fingers and spread with jam./Layer them on bottom and sides of crystal bowl./Cover with banana slices./Sprinkle with chopped walnuts./Moisten with mixture of orange juice and sherry./Set aside for at least two hours./Pour *crème anglaise* over mixture and chill for at least 4 hours./One hour before serving cover the trifle with whipped cream.

Crème Anglaise
2 cups milk
3 eggs, lightly beaten
⅓ cup sugar
1 tablespoon cornstarch
1 teaspoon vanilla

Scald milk in top of double boiler./Mix eggs with sugar to which cornstarch has been added./Pour some milk into egg mixture, then add it to the rest of the milk. Place over water that is kept just below the boiling point and stir until wooden spoon is coated./Strain into bowl and cool./Add vanilla./Chill until ready to use.

Mrs. John J. McArdle, Jr.,
Ladies' Committee

Cold Lemon Soufflé

"Lovely light dessert for a summer evening."

Serves 10-12

2 envelopes unflavored gelatin
½ cup cold water
8 eggs, separated
1 cup lemon juice
1 teaspoon salt
2 cups sugar
2 teaspoons lemon rind, grated
2 cups heavy cream

Fold 30-inch length of foil in half lengthwise./ Lightly butter inside of collar; wrap around outside of china soufflé dish that measures 6 cups to brim, forming 3-inch collar; fasten with cellophane tape./Sprinkle gelatin over cold water to soften./In double boiler top combine egg yolks, lemon juice (bottled may be used), salt, and 1 cup sugar./Cook over boiling water, stirring constantly until it coats back of spoon./Stir in gelatin and lemon rind; turn into 3-quart bowl, refrigerate until slightly thickened, stirring occasionally./Beat egg whites until they hold shape, then gradually beat in 1 cup sugar./Whip cream stiff./Pile egg whites and cream on top of lemon mixture; gently fold together./Pour into soufflé dish and refrigerate 3 hours or until firm./Serve topped with whipped cream, sprinkled with toasted slivered almonds and, if possible, surrounded with whole fresh strawberries.

Mrs. George C. Seybolt,
Ladies' Committee Associate

• **Mounds of whipped cream may be frozen on a piece of foil or waxed paper, then stored in a plastic bag.**

• **Mix fresh sliced peaches with orange juice and chopped candied ginger; sweeten to taste. Serve over sponge cake or vanilla ice cream.**

EDOUARD VUILLARD (French, 1868-1940)
The Pastry Shop, 1899. Color lithograph
Bequest of W.G. Russell Allen

Florida Orange Soufflé

"Especially good because it comes from Florida."

Serves 6

3 tablespoons flour
⅓ cup sugar
½ cup milk
1 tablespoon butter
4 egg yolks
4 tablespoons frozen orange juice concentrate, thawed but not diluted
¾ teaspoon orange rind, grated
5 egg whites
1 teaspoon salt
1 tablespoon sugar

Prepare a 2-quart soufflé dish by buttering entire inside surface and sprinkling evenly with granulated sugar./Set aside./Combine flour with ⅓ cup sugar in small saucepan; gradually blend in milk./Cook over low heat, stirring with whisk, until boiling./Continue stirring; boil 30 seconds (sauce will be very thick)./Remove from heat; beat with whisk for 2 minutes./Beat in butter and egg yolks one at a time, then orange juice concentrate and rind./Set aside./Beat egg whites and salt until soft peaks form./Add 1 tablespoon sugar gradually; beat until stiff peaks form./Fold creamy orange mixture into whites./Pour into prepared soufflé dish./Put in 425° oven, then immediately turn heat down to 375°./Bake 30 minutes, until golden brown./For darker top sprinkle with confectioner's sugar after first 20 minutes of baking.

Mrs. Richard P. C. Fitzgerald,
Ladies' Committee

• **Top fresh peaches with sweetened whipped cream and a sprinkle of crushed peanut brittle.**

• **To a fruit plate, add bananas dipped in sour cream and rolled in toasted coconut.**

Allie's Oranges

"A delectable dessert with a mysterious flavor."
Serves 6

6 large navel oranges
4 tablespoons honey
½ cup Scotch
½ cup Cointreau
pinch of salt
¼ cup sugar

Peel oranges, removing all the white membrane./Slice very thin./Mix remaining ingredients, pour over oranges, and marinate overnight./Serve slightly chilled with cookies or thin slices of pound cake.

Mrs. Samuel S. Rogers,
Ladies' Committee Associate

Oranges in Red Wine

"Delicious winter party dessert that can be made the day before and forgotten until time to serve."

Serves 8-10

8-10 navel oranges, peeled and sectioned, with membrane removed
3 tablespoons orange rind, shredded
1 cup red wine
1 cup water
¾ cup granulated sugar
2 slices lemon, including rind
2 sections tangerine (when in season)
1 stick cinnamon
2 whole cloves

Heat wine, water, sugar, lemon, cinnamon, cloves, and tangerine./Bring to boil./Remove from heat and cool./Remove tangerine, lemon, cinnamon stick, and cloves./Pour over oranges./Put into your best glass serving bowl./Pour over the cooked liquid and lay on top strips of orange rind./Cover with plastic wrap and let stand in refrigerator at least 24 hours.

Mrs. J. Denny May,
Ladies' Committee Associate

Bob Cohen's Yogurt Version of Strawberries Romanoff

"Also good on raspberries or peaches, or as a dressing for fruit salad."

Serves 2

4-5 ounces plain yogurt
2-2½ heaping teaspoons confectioner's
    sugar
2 teaspoons Grand Marnier
1 teaspoon Cognac
strawberries, washed and hulled

Stir together first 4 ingredients. (Adjust sugar and Grand Marnier according to tartness of yogurt and personal preference.)/Pour sauce over strawberries.

Mrs. Robert A. Cohen,
Ladies' Committee Associate

Whiskey Icebox Cake

"One of the easiest and most popular desserts I have ever made!"

Serves 12

2 envelopes gelatin
½ cup cold water
½ cup boiling water
6 eggs, separated
8 tablespoons whiskey (I prefer bourbon)
1 cup sugar
1 teaspoon lemon juice
2 cups heavy cream
3 packages of lady fingers, split
2 cups water with 2 tablespoons whiskey

Soak gelatin in cold water, then add boiling water to dissolve./In a large bowl beat the egg yolks until pale and thick./Add whiskey very slowly, continuing to beat mixture./Beat in sugar and add the lemon juice./Stir in the gelatin and chill briefly./Whip the cream and gently fold into the mixture./Beat the egg whites until stiff but not dry and fold them into mixture./Line the sides and bottom of a springform pan (or a charlotte mold) with lady fingers that have been dipped very lightly in whiskey and water mixture./Slowly pour the mixture into the lined pan./When filled about halfway, put in a layer of lady fingers./When filled, place another layer of lady fingers on top./Cover and chill overnight.

When ready to serve, take a long knife and run it around edge of pan, remove springform and serve./In the case of a charlotte mold, run a knife around edge and turn onto serving plate.

Anne L. Poulet,
Curator, European Decorative Arts

Frozen Lime Mousse

"A favorite at the Museum Restaurant."

Serves 10-12

3 fresh limes
6 egg yolks
½ cup sugar
3 tablespoons Rose's lime juice
1 tablespoon lime-flavored gelatin
6 tablespoons dry white wine
1 quart heavy cream
6 egg whites
¼ cup sugar
1 tablespoon brandy
green food coloring

Grate the skin of the limes, just removing the surface (should yield about 2 tablespoons rind)./Cut the limes and squeeze juice (yield-⅓ to ½ cup)./In the top of a double boiler, beat together rind, juice, egg yolks, ½ cup sugar, Rose's lime juice, gelatin, and wine./Cook until thickened, stirring constantly./Remove from heat and allow to cool./Meanwhile, beat heavy cream until it stands in peaks./Then beat 6 egg whites until stiff, gradually adding ¼ cup sugar./Fold egg whites into lime mixture, then fold in cream, brandy, and food coloring./Pile into parfait glasses and chill, or spoon into mold and freeze.

Chef Alfred Georgs,
Museum Restaurant

Poppy-Seed Mocha Torte

"A recipe brought back from my travels. The pièce de résistance at my parties."

Serves 8-10

3 eggs, separated
1 (12-ounce) can Solo poppy filling
¼ cup rum, sherry, or brandy
6 ounces raspberry jam
2 teaspoons instant coffee powder
4 teaspoons sugar
1 tablespoon cocoa
1 cup heavy cream, stiffly beaten

Beat the egg yolks until light, then mix in poppy filling./Beat the egg whites until stiff but not dry./Fold whites gently into poppy seed mixture./Pour into buttered 9-inch springform pan./Bake for 30-40 minutes at 400° or until golden brown./Remove from oven and cool completely./With a sharp knife, split the torte into two layers./Sprinkle rum or other liquor over each layer./Spread jam over the layers.

Moisten instant coffee with a little cream./Mix with sugar and cocoa and blend in the stiffly beaten cream./Spread a portion of the cream over one layer of the torte, then top with the second layer./Cover entire torte with remaining cream./Store in refrigerator briefly or in freezer for a longer period./Decorate with walnut halves.

Mrs. E. Anthony Kutten,
Museum Art Tour Coordinator

Minted Melon Mold

"I make this in a ring mold and fill the center with fresh mint."

Serves 6-8

2 tablespoons plain gelatin
1¼ cups water
1 cup sugar
½ cup fresh mint, finely chopped
1½ cups orange juice

⅓ cup lemon juice
dash of salt
melon balls cut from 1 cantaloupe

Soften gelatin in ¼ cup cold water./Boil the remaining 1 cup water with sugar 5 minutes./Add the mint./Cover and let mint steep until liquid is cool./Strain, pressing as much mint flavor through as possible./Dissolve gelatin over hot water./Add to mint liquid along with orange juice, lemon juice, and salt./When partially set, fold in the melon balls./Chill until firm.

Miss Ellen Stillman,
Ladies' Committee Associate

Jayne's Walnut Torte

"Never any left over when this is served!"

Serves 8-10

4 egg yolks
1½ cups sugar
¼ cup Wondra flour
2 teaspoons baking powder
1 teaspoon salt
4 egg whites
1 teaspoon vanilla
3 cups walnuts, chopped

Frosting
1 cup heavy cream, whipped
1 teaspoon to 1 tablespoon instant coffee
2 tablespoons sugar
1 teaspoon vanilla

Beat yolks until thick./Gradually beat in ¾ cup sugar./Mix dry ingredients./Fold into yolk mixture./Beat whites until stiff, gradually adding ¾ cup sugar./Fold yolk mixture and vanilla into whites and turn into greased 9-inch springform pan./Bake at 350° for 35-40 minutes./Cool and frost.

(Do not be alarmed if a crack appears on torte, as it will be covered by frosting.)

Mrs. Paul Bernat, Trustee

Chocolate Sheet Cake

"Scrumptious, moist, chocolate treat."

Serves 15

2 cups sugar
2 cups sifted flour
½ teaspoon salt
1 stick butter
½ cup shortening
1 cup water
6 tablespoons cocoa
2 eggs, slightly beaten
½ cup buttermilk
1 teaspoon vanilla
1 teaspoon baking soda

Sift sugar, flour, and salt./In saucepan bring butter, shortening, water, and cocoa to boil./Remove from heat and pour over dry ingredients./Mix well./Beat in eggs and other ingredients./Mix well./Pour into greased and floured 10 x 15 x 1-inch pan and bake at 325° for 30 minutes.

Icing
6 tablespoons cocoa
6 tablespoons milk
1 stick butter
1 box confectioner's sugar
1 teaspoon vanilla
1 cup broken pecans or walnuts (optional)

Make icing while cake is baking./Bring to boil cocoa, milk, and butter./Remove from heat, add *sifted* confectioner's sugar and vanilla. (Stir in nuts if added.)/Pour over cake *while it is hot.*

Mrs. Robert L. V. French,
Ladies' Committee Associate

▪ **Pour Crème de Menthe over lemon sherbet, add a sprig of fresh mint, and serve with macaroons.**

Sorbetto di Tragole (Strawberry Sherbet)

"Do not even attempt this recipe unless strawberries are very ripe and very flavorful. I know nothing else works because I've tried."

Yield: 1 quart

1 cup water
1 teaspoon sugar
1 quart very ripe fresh strawberries
juice of 2 lemons
juice of 1 orange

Boil sugar and water for 5 minutes./Remove from heat and cool./Wash berries thoroughly and hull./Reserve 6 strawberries for later use./Purée remaining berries in food processor or blender./Add lemon and orange juice and cooled sugar syrup to purée./Pour into shallow baking pan and place in freezer./As sherbet begins to freeze around edges, stir it until it is smooth./Repeat this process 2 or 3 times./When almost solid, beat with an electric beater until smooth./Slice the reserved berries and stir into the sherbet./Refreeze.

Mrs. Martha B. Leonard,
Ladies' Committee

Southern Comfort

"It's not what you think! An old southern recipe served me by an old southern colonel."

Serves 12 or more

1 quart vanilla ice cream
1 quart milk
1 quart rum, dark or golden

Mix in punch bowl over a cake of ice.

Mrs. William E. Park,
Ladies' Committee Associate

Mint Sherbet

"A family recipe. Delicious served plain or over fresh fruit."

Yield: about 1½ pints

1 cup sugar
2 cups water
¼ cup lemon juice
½ cup mint leaves, bruised
1 egg white, beaten
green coloring

Boil the sugar and water for five minutes, then add the lemon juice and mint./Cool and strain./Add green coloring, if desired./Pour into tray and freeze to consistency of mush./Fold in beaten egg white and freeze.

Mrs. Edward Wagenknecht,
Ladies' Committee Associate

Mississippi Mud

"Like cutting velvet! A superb dessert."

Serves 10-12

2 cups flour
1 teaspoon baking soda
1 pinch salt
1¾ cups coffee (ready made)
¼ cup bourbon
5 ounces unsweetened chocolate
2 sticks butter, cut into pieces
2 cups sugar
2 eggs, slightly beaten
1 teaspoon vanilla

Butter bundt pan and dust with cocoa./Sift together flour, baking soda, and salt./In a double boiler melt and mix together until smooth coffee, bourbon, chocolate, and butter./Add sugar./Cool for 3 minutes./Place mixture in mixing bowl./Add flour mixture ½ cup at a time./Beat at medium speed for 1 minute./Add eggs and vanilla./Beat until smooth./Pour batter into pan and bake at 275° for 1½ hours./Test with toothpick./Cool completely in pan./Serve with whipped cream.

Susan Jaeger, Gallery Instructor

Raspberry Torte

"A favorite recipe for over 10 years."

Serves 18-20

Crust
1¼ cups flour
¼ cup sugar
¼ teaspoon salt
1 cup butter (or margarine), chilled

Combine flour, sugar, and salt./Cut in chilled butter until mixture resembles coarse crumbs./Pat in bottom of 13 x 9 x 2-inch pan./Bake at 350° until lightly browned (15-18 minutes)./Cool.

Filling
3 tablespoons cornstarch
1 cup sugar
2 (10-ounce) packages frozen red
  raspberries, thawed

Combine cornstarch and sugar in saucepan./Add the raspberries and cook, stirring constantly, until mixture comes to a boil and is clear./Cool slightly and pour over crust./Chill.

Topping
1 (10-ounce) package large marshmallows
1 cup milk
1 cup heavy cream, whipped

Place marshmallows and milk in saucepan./Cook over low heat, stirring frequently, until the marshmallows melt./Cool./Fold whipped cream into marshmallow mixture./Spread over chilled raspberry filling./Chill.

Mrs. F. Thomas Westcott,
Ladies' Committee

Raspberry Parfait

"A quick and easy dessert with a delicious sweet-tart taste."

Serves 4-6

1 small can frozen lemonade
1 cup water
¼ cup minute tapioca
¼ cup sugar
1 package good-quality frozen raspberries

Bring the lemonade and water to a boil./Add the tapioca and sugar and cook until clear (about 5 minutes)./Stir in the frozen raspberries and spoon into parfait glasses./Chill in refrigerator./Serve with whipped cream.

*Mrs. Robert W. Meserve,
Ladies' Committee Associate*

Note: Frozen strawberries may be substituted for raspberries.

Ann Decaneas's Ravani

"A delicious Greek lemon sponge cake."

Yield: 24 pieces

6 eggs, beaten
1 cup sugar
1 cup flour
3 teaspoons baking powder
1 teaspoon vanilla

Beat eggs and sugar until thick, and add vanilla./Fold in flour with baking powder./Pour into greased 9½ x 13-inch pan./Bake at 350° for about 30 minutes or until golden brown./Cool./Cut into 24 medium-sized diamond-shaped pieces./Pour hot syrup over pieces evenly.

Syrup
1½ cups water
1½ cups sugar
juice and grated rind of 1 lemon
1 teaspoon vanilla

Boil water, sugar, and lemon juice for 5 minutes./Add 1 teaspoon vanilla./Tastes better if left in the pan overnight so that the syrup is absorbed.

*Mrs. Frank Zervas,
Ladies' Committee Associate*

Middle-Ages Almond Cheesecake

"Quite different from the usual cheesecake. Delicious!"

Serves 8

1 cup less 2 level tablespoons sugar
¼ cup butter
1 pound cream cheese
¼ cup sifted flour
2 tablespoons honey
5 eggs, separated (whites beaten stiff but not dry)
½ cup light cream
¼ teaspoon almond extract
1 teaspoon vanilla extract
½ cup blanched almonds, finely chopped

Topping
¼ cup light brown sugar
1 teaspoon cinnamon
¼ cup almonds, finely chopped

Cream butter and sugar./Beat in cheese until fluffy./Blend in flour and honey, then the egg yolks, beating well./Add cream and extracts./Lightly fold in beaten egg whites./Fold in the chopped almonds./Pour into well-buttered 9-inch springform pan./Sprinkle with topping mixture./Set on low rack in preheated 325° oven and bake 1 hour./Turn off heat and cool in oven for 1 hour.

Jane H. Bryant, Gallery Instructor

▪ **Swirl brandy or your favorite liqueur through French vanilla ice cream. Spoon into parfait glasses.**

Cold Pineapple Soufflé

*"Reminiscent of Piña Colada. A big hit
when I serve it."*

Serves 6-8

7 egg yolks
½ cup superfine sugar
4 egg whites
1 cup crushed pineapple, well drained
¼ cup cream of coconut
2 envelopes gelatin
¼ cup dark rum
½ pint heavy cream

Encircle a 6-cup soufflé dish with a 3-inch aluminum foil collar./Butter and sprinkle with
granulated sugar the entire inside surface./In a
mixing bowl, beat egg yolks and sugar until
very light, fluffy, and lemon colored./Add the
pineapple and cream of coconut./In a small
saucepan sprinkle the gelatin over the rum./
When spongy, dissolve over hot water./Cool
and add to the pineapple mixture./Beat the
egg whites until stiff./In a separate bowl beat
cream until it mounds./Fold the cream into
the pineapple mixture, then gently fold in egg
whites./Spoon carefully into soufflé dish./
Chill for several hours./Remove collar carefully to give effect of a risen soufflé./Prepare
the same day to be served.

Mrs. Malcolm L. Trayser,
Ladies' Committee Associate

Chinese Almond Jelly

*"A delicious light dessert that complements
any Chinese dinner."*

Serves 6

2 packages unflavored gelatin
1 cup plus 2 tablespoons water
1 cup milk
¾ cup sugar
1 teaspoon almond extract

Syrup
¼ cup sugar
1 cup water

Garnish
6 slices pineapple
6 cherries

Sprinkle gelatin on 2 tablespoons water to
soften./Bring 1 cup of water to boil./Add gelatin and stir until dissolved./Stir in milk, sugar,
and almond extract./Pour into shallow pan./
Chill in refrigerator./Bring sugar and water to
boil to make syrup./Chill in refrigerator./Cut
almond jelly into diamond shapes and place in
serving dish./Pour syrup over it and garnish
with pineapple and cherries.

Jane H. Bryant, Gallery Instructor

Grand Marnier Sauce

"Forget all the Romanoffs. This is the best."

Yield: 2½ cups

5 egg yolks
½ cup superfine sugar
2 tablespoons Grand Marnier

1 cup heavy cream
2 tablespoons superfine sugar
2 tablespoons Grand Marnier

In a bowl set over a saucepan of hot water, beat
the egg yolks with ½ cup sugar until the mixture is light and ribbons when beater is lifted./
Remove the bowl from the pan and beat in 2
tablespoons Grand Marnier./Set the bowl in a
bowl filled with ice and whisk mixture until
cool.

In another bowl beat heavy cream until it
holds soft peaks./Beat in 2 tablespoons sugar
and continue beating until it forms stiff
peaks./Fold the cream into the egg yolk mixture with 2 more tablespoons Grand Marnier.

Serve with fresh raspberries or strawberries.

Mrs. Mayo A. Shattuck,
Ladies' Committee Associate

Nockerl

"A sublime dessert from Salzburg, city of music and marionettes, which we have adapted for the American kitchen."

Serves 4-8

4 egg yolks
¼ cup flour
⅛ teaspoon salt
8 egg whites
½ cup sugar
1 teaspoon vanilla
3 tablespoons butter
confectioner's sugar

Beat egg yolks until light and lemon colored./ Add flour mixed with salt, gradually./Beat very well./Beat egg whites until fairly stiff and gradually add sugar while continuing to beat./ Add vanilla./Beat until quite stiff./Fold the egg-yolk mixture into the beaten whites./Heat butter in 12-inch iron skillet (do not brown butter)./With large wooden spoon, place 8 mounds of batter into skillet./Cook on top of stove until the mounds are lightly browned on the bottom./Place the skillet in 250° oven and cook about 10 minutes or until the top is lightly browned./Remove mounds to serving plates./Dust with confectioner's sugar and serve immediately.

Clementine Brown,
Manager, Public Information
(with thanks to Libby
Alsberg of Marblehead)

Rum Sauce

"Forget the calories. This is absolutely devastating and much better than hard sauce."

Yield: about 2½ cups

2 egg yolks
1 cup powdered sugar
6 tablespoons dark rum
1 cup heavy cream
1 tablespoon vanilla
nutmeg

Beat the egg yolks together with the sugar until the sugar is well dissolved./Slowly add the rum and beat well./Whip the cream until it holds its shape, adding the vanilla as you go along./Gently fold the egg mixture into the whipped cream and refrigerate./Sprinkle a little nutmeg on top before serving.

Mrs. Malcolm L. Trayser,
Ladies' Committee Associate

Never-Fail Chocolate Sauce

"If you follow these instructions, the chocolate sauce never sugars and remains soft and creamy."

Yield: 1 pint

1 (13-ounce) can evaporated milk
2 cups sugar
3 squares unsweetened chocolate
1 teaspoon vanilla

Combine all ingredients in a saucepan and bring to a boil, stirring constantly./Boil for 5 minutes, continuing to stir./Remove from stove, stir in vanilla and beat with an egg beater for 1 minute.

Mrs. Frank G. Allen,
Ladies' Committee Associate

KITAGAWA UTAMARO (Japanese, 1753 – 1806)
Woman Holding a Sake Cup. Woodblock print. Spaulding Collection

Tea Time

Cookies while You Sleep

"A long-time favorite."

Yield: 40

2 egg whites
¼ teaspoon cream of tartar
¼ cup sugar
1 teaspoon vanilla
¼ teaspoon almond extract
¼ teaspoon salt
1 cup pecans or walnuts, chopped
¾ cup chocolate or butterscotch bits

Preheat oven to 350°./Beat egg whites until firm./Add salt and cream of tartar./Continue beating until egg whites are stiff./Very gradually add sugar and extracts./Beat until shiny and stiff./Fold in nuts and bits./Drop by teaspoon on well-greased pan (they do not spread)./Turn off heat and leave in oven overnight./Do not open door until morning!

Miss Elizabeth B. Storer,
Ladies' Committee Associate

Chocolate Crunch Squares

"A favorite of my family. Simple, delicious!"
Yield: 2 dozen or more

2 squares unsweetened chocolate
½ cup shortening
1 cup sugar
2 eggs
pinch of salt
½ cup sifted flour
1 teaspoon vanilla
1 cup walnuts or pecans, finely chopped

Melt chocolate and shortening together./Add sugar./Beat eggs in one at a time./Stir in salt, flour, and vanilla./Spread thin with spatula in buttered and floured large cookie pan./Sprinkle top with nuts./Bake 15-18 minutes at 350°./Cut immediately into long rectangles and remove to cooling racks.

Mrs. Victor A. Lutnicki,
Ladies' Committee

Easy Little Cookies

"Melt-in-your-mouth goodness."

Yield: 80

½ cup butter
1 cup light brown sugar, lightly packed
1 teaspoon vanilla
1 egg
¾ cup sifted flour
1 teaspoon baking powder
½ teaspoon salt
½ cup pecans, finely chopped

Cream butter; add sugar, vanilla, and egg./Beat until light./Add sifted dry ingredients and nuts./Drop by scant teaspoonfuls onto ungreased Teflon cookie sheet at least 3 inches apart (they spread)./Bake at 400° for 5 minutes./Cool 1 or 2 minutes, then remove to rack.

Mrs. William A. Thompson,
Ladies' Committee Associate

Clove Balls

"Marvelous with tea or anytime!"

Yield: 48

1 cup butter or margarine, softened
½ cup sugar
½ teaspoon ground mace
¼ teaspoon ground cloves
2 teaspoons vanilla
1 large egg yolk
2½ cups sifted all-purpose flour
whole cloves
confectioner's sugar, sifted

Cream butter, sugar, spices, and vanilla./Beat in egg yolk./Stir in flour./Chill dough 1 hour or until stiff enough to handle./Make 1-inch balls./Place 1 inch apart on ungreased cookie sheet./Insert whole clove in center of each./Bake at 325° for 20 minutes or until lightly brown (do not bake too brown)./Roll in sugar./Store in airtight container.

Mrs. Robert Morgan,
Ladies' Committee Associate

GEORGES BRAQUE (French, 1882–1963)
Teapot and Lemons, 1947. Color lithograph
Bequest of W.G. Russell Allen

Detail from interior of a punchbowl. Chelsea porcelain, ca. 1760
Bequest of Forsyth Wickes; Forsyth Wickes Collection

Lemon Bars

"Delicious served as tea cakes or can be cut into larger pieces and served with whipped cream as dessert."

Yield: 16 large
(36 small) bars

1 cup flour
½ cup butter
¼ cup powdered sugar

Mix the above and pat into an 8 x 8-inch glass pan./Bake 20 minutes at 350°./Cool 10 minutes. While the above is baking, combine:

2 eggs, beaten slightly
½ teaspoon baking powder
2 tablespoons fresh lemon juice
grated rind of 1 lemon
1 cup sugar
2 tablespoons flour

Mix well and pour onto crust./Bake for 25 minutes at 350°./Cut into bars. (Sprinkle with powdered sugar if you wish.)

Mrs. Edward Wagenknecht,
Ladies' Committee Associate

Pecan Balls

"You'll make these again and again."

Yield: 60-75 balls

½ pound butter
½ cup sugar
2 cups flour
2 teaspoons vanilla
2 cups pecans, finely chopped

Cream butter and sugar./Add other ingredients./Shape into balls./Bake on ungreased cookie sheet at 300° for 40 minutes./While warm, roll in powdered sugar.

Mrs. Lester A. Steinberg,
Ladies' Committee

Danish Cinnamon Sticks

"This is one of my grandmother's Danish Christmas cookie recipes, but they taste good all year round, especially with tea."

Yield: 200 or more

Dough
¼ pound butter
1 cup sugar
2 cups flour
1 tablespoon cinnamon
1 egg, lightly beaten

Cream together the butter and sugar./Sift the flour and cinnamon and add to butter-sugar mixture; mix well./Add the egg and mix thoroughly.

Divide dough into 5 sections and chill.

Topping
½ cup sugar
2½ teaspoons cinnamon

Mix the sugar and cinnamon. (To apply, use empty spice jar with shaker top.)

On floured surface, with floured rolling pin, roll out dough, one section at a time, as thin as possible./From this recipe, you will have a total of 220 cookies if they are rolled as thin as my grandmother's were./Add scraps from preceding section of dough to the next section and work them in./This softens chilled dough a bit and makes rolling easier.

Cut into strips 1 x 3 inches and place close together on buttered cookie sheet./Sprinkle liberally with topping mixture. Bake in 350° oven./Check in 5 minutes and remove cookies when barely brown on *bottom*./Cinnamon disguises browning of tops./Some may cook faster than others on the same sheet./They are not crisp when removed from sheet, but they crisp when cool.

Mrs. James A. Marsh,
Ladies' Committee Associate

Japanese Almond Cookies

"Serve as dessert with any oriental dinner, or as tea cookies. Light and tasty."

Yield: 3 dozen

1⅔ cups whole blanched almonds
2 egg whites
dash of salt
⅔ cup sugar

Spread 1½ cups almonds in shallow baking pan./Bake 10 minutes at 350° until toasted and nicely browned./Finely grind almonds, using food processor or blender./In medium bowl, beat egg whites with salt until foamy./Add sugar, 2 tablespoons at a time, beating well after each addition./Continue beating until stiff peaks form when beater is raised./Fold in ground nuts./Mixture should be thick and hold its shape./Drop by heaping teaspoonfuls, 1 inch apart, on well-greased cookie sheets. Top each with one of remaining whole almonds./Bake at 350° for 7-10 minutes or just until lightly browned./Remove from cookie sheet at once./Cool on wire rack.

Mrs. John K. Bryant,
Ladies' Committee Associate

Kris Kringles

"Have made these for our annual eggnog party at Christmas for at least 25 years."

Yield: 36 cookies

½ cup butter
¼ cup sugar
1 egg yolk
1 tablespoon orange peel, grated
1 teaspoon lemon peel, grated
1 teaspoon lemon juice
1 cup flour
⅛ teaspoon salt
1 egg white, slightly beaten
½ cup pecans or walnuts, finely chopped
18 candied cherries, cut in half

Cream shortening and sugar thoroughly, add egg yolk, orange and lemon peels, and lemon juice./Beat thoroughly./Stir in flour and salt./ Chill until firm./Form small balls about ½ inch in diameter./Dip in egg white and then in finely chopped nuts./Press half a candied cherry in the center of each cookie./Bake at 325° about 20 minutes.

Mrs. Shattuck W. Osborne,
Ladies' Committee Associate

Strawberry Rounds

"Serve for tea or with a fruit or champagne punch."

Cut rounds of bread from thin slices./Spread with hard sauce made with confectioner's or superfine sugar./Top each round with a whole strawberry.

Mrs. William E. Park,
Ladies' Committee Associate

ANONYMOUS CHINESE (T'ang Dynasty, 7th century)
Wine cup with high foot. White porcelain
Charles B. Hoyt Collection

Almond Diamonds

"Nice with tea on a winter afternoon."

Yield: 6 dozen

1 cup butter, softened
1 cup sugar
1 egg, separated
1 teaspoon almond extract
2 cups sifted all-purpose flour
½ cup blanched almonds, sliced
1 tablespoon sugar
¼ teaspoon cinnamon

Beat butter and sugar until fluffy and light./
Stir in egg yolk and almond extract./Stir in
flour./Dough will be stiff./Turn dough into
ungreased Teflon 15 x 10 x 1-inch jelly-roll
pan./Spread evenly to edge with spatula./Beat
egg white until foamy./Spread evenly over
cookie dough./Sprinkle nuts on top./Combine
sugar with cinnamon; sprinkle over nuts.

Bake at 350° for 25-30 minutes or until lightly
browned./Remove from oven; cool in pan on
wire rack for 10 minutes./Cut into 8 lengthwise
strips, then into 12 diagonal cuts to form diamond shapes./Cool thoroughly in pan./
Remove carefully with spatula.

Mrs. Ulf B. Heide,
Ladies' Committee

Spritz

"A delicious cookie recipe from an
old Swedish friend."

Yield: 4-5 dozen

2 cups flour
1 teaspoon baking powder
1 egg, beaten slightly
1 cup butter, at room temperature
½ cup sugar
2 teaspoons almond flavor

Sift flour, then measure./Add baking powder
to egg./Cream butter and sugar./Add egg and
beat well./Add almond flavor./Stir in flour./
Use cookie press with any design but tradi-
tionally the Swedish make these cookies in the
shape of an "S"./Bake about 10 minutes at 350°
on ungreased cookie sheet.

Mrs. Charles A. Whitney,
Ladies' Committee

Brandy Balls

"A hit on the cookie plate at parties."

Yield: 45-50 balls

2 cups vanilla wafers, crumbed (1 package)
1 cup pecans, finely chopped
1 cup mixed candied fruit, finely cut
1 cup confectioner's sugar
2 tablespoons cocoa
2 tablespoons white corn syrup
½ cup brandy (or rum or Cointreau)

Roll crumbs very fine./Add the other ingredients and mix well./Shape by teaspoonfuls into
firm balls./Roll in granulated sugar./Store in
tightly covered container for at least one week
so that flavors will blend.

Mrs. Shattuck W. Osborne,
Ladies' Committee Associate

ANONYMOUS CHINESE (Ch'ing Dynasty;
Yung-cheng Period, 1723 –1735)
Wine cup (Ching-te-chen ware). Porcelain
Gift of Mr. and Mrs. Paul Bernat

A Medley of Sauces, Preserves & Confections

Cook's Marinade

"Marinate any cut of beef or chicken in this sauce before grilling over charcoal."

Yield: 1⅓ cups

1 cup stale beer
¼ cup soy sauce
½ teaspoon Worcestershire sauce
1 tablespoon dry mustard
1 teaspoon ground ginger
5 tablespoons marmalade (orange is best)
2 large cloves garlic, crushed
½ teaspoon salt
¼ teaspoon pepper, freshly ground

Mrs. Kevit R. Cook,
Ladies' Committee Associate

Specialty-of-the-House Barbecue Sauce

"Delicious for chicken, pork chops, spare ribs."

Yield: about 1 pint

1 (8-ounce) can tomato sauce
½ cup olive oil
½ cup orange juice
¼ cup vinegar
1½ teaspoons dried oregano
1 teaspoon salt
6 peppercorns
1 clove garlic, minced

In a large jar with screw top combine all ingredients, cover, and shake vigorously./Keep in refrigerator until ready to use./Can be used for marinating chicken (overnight in refrigerator is best) or just for brushing on chicken, pork chops, or ribs as they are grilled.

Mrs. Richard C. Anderson,
Ladies' Committee

Emerald Cream

"Nice with cold chicken."

Serves 6

1 quart milk
2 teaspoons salt
½ teaspoon pepper
1 teaspoon dried tarragon
½ teaspoon dill
6 eggs
2 egg yolks
1 tablespoon flour
¼ cup warm water
1 tablespoon parsley, minced
¼ cup watercress, minced
¼ cup scallion greens, minced
2 teaspoons Worcestershire sauce
few drops Tabasco
2 tablespoons Bourbon or Scotch whiskey
2 teaspoons oil

In non-aluminum pot, heat milk with salt and pepper./In a 2-quart bowl, crush tarragon and dill between fingers until powdery fine./Add eggs and yolks./Beat until light./When milk almost reaches boiling point, slowly pour into beaten egg while beating *rapidly.*/Return this mixture to pot.

Stir water into flour until smooth and add to pot./Cook on low heat 1 minute, while adding parsley, watercress, scallions, Worcestershire, and Tabasco./Remove from heat and add whiskey.

Lightly oil 6-cup soufflé dish./Pour in liquid and place dish in pan containing hot water to cover half of dish./Bake at 350° for 1½ hours./Cream is done when it puffs slightly, has crack in top, and begins to pull away from sides (knife inserted comes out clean)./Herbs will float to surface, baked to a green topping./Cool, then chill well. (Can be made a day in advance – no longer or it loses its delicacy.)

Mrs. William M. Hogan, Jr.,
Ladies' Committee Associate

Hilton Head Island Green Pepper Jelly

"Delicious with meat, fowl, and fish. Also good as an hors d'oeuvre *with cream cheese on crackers."*

Yield: 6 (8-ounce) glasses

3 large thick green peppers
6½ cups sugar
1½ cups cider vinegar
¼ fresh hot red pepper or 2-4 tablespoons hot crushed red pepper
1 (6-ounce) bottle Certo
green coloring

Remove seeds from green peppers, grind fine./ Mix juice and pulp (¾ cup) with sugar, vinegar, and hot pepper./Bring to boil, add Certo and boil, stirring constantly./Pour through fine strainer, skim, and add a few drops of green food coloring (if you wish it hotter, add a little cayenne)./Pour into sterilized jelly glasses.

Mrs. Sterling F. Myrick,
Ladies' Committee Associate

Mustard Sauce

"An old family recipe. We serve it with thinly sliced ham and baking powder biscuits for make-it-yourself hors d'oeuvres.*"*

Yield: 1¼ cups

1 tablespoon butter
1 tablespoon flour
2 tablespoons dry mustard
3 tablespoons sugar (or less)
⅓ cup boiling water
1 teaspoon salt
2 teaspoons horseradish
⅓ cup vinegar
⅓ cup mayonnaise

Melt the butter in a heavy saucepan./Add the flour and cook for one minute./Add the mustard, sugar, water, salt, and horseradish, stirring constantly./Add the vinegar and mix well./Cook for 10 minutes; cool slightly and then whip in the mayonnaise.

Mrs. Malcolm L. Trayser,
Ladies' Committee Associate

Green Mayonnaise

"A favorite crudités dip. Good too with cold fish or shrimp, or as a dressing for three-bean salad."

Yield: 1 pint

1 egg
1 tablespoon fresh lemon juice
¾ teaspoon salt
¼ teaspoon white pepper, freshly ground
1½ cups olive oil
6 sprigs parsley
4 green onions, chopped
1 teaspoon dried chervil (or 1 tablespoon fresh)
1 teaspoon dried tarragon (or 1 tablespoon fresh)
1 teaspoon dried dill (or 1 tablespoon fresh)
1 teaspoon dried chives (or 1 tablespoon fresh)

Place egg, lemon juice, salt, and pepper in processor./Using metal blade, start motor./ Begin pouring in oil very slowly through feed tube drop by drop, then a very thin stream until all oil is used./Stop motor./Add herbs; process briefly until well mixed, scraping down sides of container./Taste for lemon juice and salt./Chill. (Keeps well; the flavor improves.)

Larry Salmon,
Former Curator, Textiles

Blender Mayonnaise

"This one is really foolproof."

Yield: 2½ cups

2 extra-large eggs
1 teaspoon salt
1 teaspoon dry mustard
½ teaspoon paprika
2 tablespoons lemon juice
2 tablespoons vinegar
2 cups oil

Put the eggs and seasonings in blender and whir to mix until blended./Stop the motor./ Add lemon juice and begin processing./ Remove cover, and *very* slowly pour in half the oil./Add the vinegar and the rest of oil slowly, whirring all the time.

Miss Ellen Stillman,
Ladies' Committee Associate

Peanut Butter

"Make your own for best flavor."

Yield: about 2 cups

2 cups roasted, salted peanuts (not dry
    roasted)
1 stick butter, at room temperature
2 tablespoons molasses
½ cup sunflower seeds

Put peanuts through food processor feed tube with motor running and run until peanuts turn to peanut butter(about 3-5 minutes)./With motor still running add butter gradually and then molasses./Finally, add sunflower seeds and process until they are partially chopped up./Keeps well in refrigerator but must be removed well before serving for butter to soften./Can also be made with unsalted, roasted peanuts, adding salt to taste.

Larry Salmon,
Former Curator, Textiles

Sauce à la Henriette

"A tart, spicy sauce, delicious over steak."

Yield: about ⅔ cup

1 egg yolk
¼ teaspoon salt
1½ teaspoons lemon juice
2 tablespoons cold water
6 tablespoons butter
2 tablespoons tomato purée
1 teaspoon Worcestershire sauce

Beat first four ingredients together./In the top of a double boiler, melt 2 tablespoons butter./ Add egg yolk mixture, stirring constantly./ Cook over hot water until thickened, continuing to stir./Add 2 tablespoons butter, then 2 tablespoons more of butter, stirring each time until butter melts./Blend in tomato purée and Worcestershire sauce.

Evalyn Beckwith, Resource Development

Apricot Chutney

"Delicious with poultry or pork."

1 cup dried apricots, chopped
¼ cup water
¼ cup honey
2 apples, pared, cored, and diced
¼ cup golden raisins
1 clove garlic, minced
1 onion, diced
juice of ½ lemon
½ teaspoon ground ginger
grated rind of ½ lemon
dash of Tabasco (optional)
salt and pepper

Simmer all ingredients 5-10 minutes or until liquid is absorbed./Adjust seasoning./Let it stand refrigerated 24 hours before serving./ Serve at room temperature.

Mrs. Selwyn A. Kudisch,
Ladies' Committee

Cooked Crackers

"Serve these crisp crackers with soup, salad, or cheese."

Soak individual saltines in ice water to cover for 7 minutes./Drain and lift carefully with a spatula and place ½ inch apart on ungreased cookie sheet./Brush with melted butter and bake for 10 minutes at 500°./Turn to 375° and continue baking for ½ hour or until brown and crisp.

Mrs. Fred Glimp,
Ladies' Committee Associate

Chatham Chutney

"A favorite for Christmas giving and home consumption! Fun to prepare. The aroma is heavenly."

Yield: 6-8 quarts

12 pounds firm peaches
½ pound green or red peppers, seeded and chopped
⅛ pound green ginger, chopped
2 cloves garlic, mashed
3 pounds raisins (seedless)

Blanch peaches in boiling water for easy peeling; pare and slice./Mix with remaining ingredients.

Make syrup by boiling:

2 quarts cider vinegar
4 pounds dark brown sugar
6 ounces mustard seed
1 tablespoon salt

Combine all ingredients in large heavy kettle and celery; simmer 10-15 minutes longer, uncovered, or until mixture is thick./Cool and refrigerate.

Mrs. Frank Zervas,
Ladies' Committee Associate

Cranberry Chutney

"Delicious with poultry. Keeps in refrigerator for weeks."

Yield: 45 ounces

4 cups (1 pound) cranberries
1 cup seedless raisins
1⅔ cups sugar
1 tablespoon cinnamon
1½ teaspoons ginger
¼ teaspoon cloves
1 cup water
½ cup onion, chopped
1 medium-sized apple, pared, cored, and chopped
½ cup celery, thinly sliced

Combine cranberries, raisins, sugar, cinnamon, ginger, cloves, and water in a large covered saucepan./Cook 15 minutes until berries pop and mixture thickens./Stir in onion, apple, and celery; simmer 10-15 minutes longer, uncovered, or until mixture is thick./Cool and refrigerate.

Mrs. Frank Zervas,
Ladies' Committee Associate

Spiced Pears

"I always triple this recipe. A delicious accompaniment for meat."

1 (29-ounce) can pear halves (6-10 halves)
6 whole cloves
¼ cup burgundy wine
⅛ cup vinegar
¼ cup honey

Drain pears, reserving ½ cup syrup./Put syrup in saucepan with remaining ingredients, bring to boil, and add pears./Simmer 10 minutes./Serve warm or chilled as meat accompaniment. (Keeps in refrigerator for weeks.)

Mrs. Frank Zervas,
Ladies' Committee Associate

Peach Chutney

"This is an excellent condiment for any curry dish."

Yield: 1 quart

1 (11-ounce) can Elberta peaches
¾ cup sugar
2 pieces crystallized ginger, thinly sliced
½ teaspoon vinegar
½ teaspoon curry
¼ teaspoon powdered ginger
salt
1 (9-ounce) bottle Major Grey's chutney

Drain the peaches and chop into small pieces./ Put the juice in a saucepan with sugar and ginger./Boil down at high temperature for 3 minutes./Add peaches, vinegar, curry, powdered ginger, and salt./Simmer 10 minutes, then blend in chutney.

Mrs. Donald J. Hurley,
Ladies' Committee Associate

Strawberry Jam

"In June we pick a big basketful of large, deep red strawberries and then have the fun of making this delicious jam from my mother's recipe."

Yield: 6 jelly jars

4 cups strawberries
2 cups sugar

In a wide-bottomed heavy pan, layer strawberries and sugar and let them stand, covered, for 12 hours./Uncover and bring rapidly to the boiling point./Boil quickly for 15 minutes./ Pour the jam into a large bowl and let stand for 2 days, stirring gently several times a day./ Spoon the jam into hot sterilized jars and cover at once with melted paraffin.

Mrs. Robert L. M. Ahern,
Ladies' Committee Associate

Rhubarb Jam

"A friend gave us a rhubarb plant, for some years now a "heavy feeder" in one corner of our rose garden. But the rhubarb has been worth the effort, if only for this recipe, which came with the gift."

Yield: about 6 jelly jars

5 cups rhubarb, cut in 1-inch pieces
1 cup crushed pineapple, drained
4 cups sugar
1 package strawberry gelatin

To the rhubarb add pineapple and sugar and let it stand for 30 minutes./Then slowly bring to a boil and boil for 15 minutes, stirring constantly./Remove from heat./Stir in the strawberry gelatin./Pour jam into hot sterile jars and seal with melted paraffin.

Mrs. Robert L. M. Ahern,
Ladies' Committee Associate

Note: A wide, flat-bottomed heavy pan is best for jam and jelly making.

Plum Conserve

"I can still see my mother making this."

Yield: 24 half-pints

7 pounds Italian blue plums, pitted
6 pounds sugar
2 pounds seeded raisins
2 oranges, chopped
1 cup walnuts, chopped

Bring all ingredients except nuts to a full rolling boil and cook for 40 minutes, being careful that mixture does not burn./Add walnuts./ Pour into sterilized jars and cover with paraffin. (A dishwasher will sterilize the jars.)

Carol Howard, Gallery Instructor

BRIGHTON.

AMERIC.
FRUITS AND F

ANONYMOUS AMERICAN. *Brighton* (grapes). Stencil and watercolor from D.M. Dewey's *Nurseryman's Pocket Book of Specimen Fruit and Flowers*, 1875. Gift of Mrs. Alan Tawse

Uncooked Fudge

"Sinfully rich and delicious!"

Yield: 64 pieces

4 squares unsweetened chocolate
2 tablespoons butter
¼ teaspoon salt
1 teaspoon vanilla
1 pound confectioner's sugar, sifted
⅓ cup milk
1 cup Brazil nuts or pecans, chopped

Melt chocolate and butter over hot water./Stir in salt and vanilla./Stir in sugar, alternating with milk, keeping pan over hot water./ Remove from heat and stir in nuts./Pour into buttered 8-inch square pan, smoothing top./ Decorate with more nuts if desired./Let stand several hours and cut into squares.

Carol Howard,
Gallery Instructor

Taipei Pecans

"We had these in Taipei. I learned from sign language how to make them. They are slightly sweet and delicious."

Yield: 3 cups

3 cups pecan halves
water
1 cup sugar
2 cups oil for deep frying

Bring 2 quarts water to a boil./Add pecans, simmer 11 minutes, and drain (this removes bitterness from nuts)./In saucepan, combine sugar and 2 cups water./Add pecans./Simmer 11 minutes more./Pour off syrup and dry pecans on paper towels./Heat oil in shallow pan./Deep-fry pecans 7 minutes or until golden./Drain on paper towels./Pecans will be crisp when cool.

Mrs. George N. Proctor,
Ladies' Committee Associate

Mother's Pralines

"These have been a Christmas tradition in our home for as long as I can remember."

Yield: 40

2 cups granulated sugar
¾ cup light brown sugar
1¼ cups milk
3 tablespoons white corn syrup
1 stick butter
1 teaspoon vanilla
2½ cups pecan halves

Put the white and brown sugar, milk, and corn syrup into a heavy pot./Cook on medium-high heat, stirring occasionally, until a soft ball forms when a teaspoonful is dropped into cool water or until a candy thermometer reads 240°./Remove from heat and add butter and vanilla./Beat by hand or with a hand mixer until the mixture is glazed./Add the pecans and beat by hand so as not to break the nuts./ When the mixture thickens, drop onto waxed paper to harden./Work quickly, as the pralines should be creamy and not sugary./If the mixture hardens before you are finished, carefully reheat./Store in an airtight container./

Mrs. Clarence A. Kemper,
Ladies' Committee

Beverages

Iced Tea

"Keep a pitcher of this in the refrigerator for summer refreshment."

Yield: 4½ quarts

4 quarts water
6 teabags
6 teaspoons sugar
fresh mint, bruised
1 (6-ounce) can frozen orange juice
½ (6-ounce) can frozen limeade
½ (6-ounce) can frozen lemonade

Bring water to a boil./Remove from heat and steep tea, sugar, and mint for 15 minutes./ Strain and add juices./Mix thoroughly and chill.

Mrs. I. W. Colburn,
Ladies' Committee Associate

Champagne Punch

"When your party calls for champagne punch, sample this for comparison with other recipes. This recipe is a family tradition for christenings, graduations, and holiday house parties."

juice of 2 oranges
juice of 2 lemons
½ cup superfine sugar
1 cup light rum
1 cup pineapple juice
2 bottles champagne
1 bottle soda water
½ basket strawberries or raspberries

In a large punch bowl, pour the first 5 ingredients over a block of ice./Stir gently and pour in the champagne and soda water./Garnish with strawberries and raspberries.

Mrs. Roger H. McCoy,
Ladies' Committee

Frosted Rum Delight

"Easy daiquiri-like drink."

Serves 4

1 pint mixed sherbet (lemon and lime, lemon and pineapple, etc.)
4 jiggers light rum

Buzz in blender and serve.

Mrs. John Halford,
Ladies' Committee Associate

Café Brûlot

"A taste of New Orleans. Unforgettable!"

Serves 10-12

30 tiny sugar cubes (Domino Dots)
5 or 6 whole cloves
1 stick of whole cinnamon, broken
thin peeling of half an orange, cut in a long strip
thin peeling of half a lemon, cut in a long strip
1 cup cognac
1 quart strong hot coffee

Before the party, put the sugar, spices and peel into a *brûlot* (or an oven-proof) bowl./When ready to serve, heat and add the cognac./Turn the lights down low and ignite the cognac./ Stir a few moments with a flourish, but not so long as to destroy the alcohol./Pour in the hot coffee slowly and the flame will disappear./ Ladle into *brûlot* or demitasse cups.

Mrs. Clarence A. Kemper,
Ladies' Committee

- **To after-dinner coffee, add lemon peel soaked in rum.**

- **Add crushed cardamom seeds to after-dinner coffee for delicious flavor.**

ANONYMOUS AMERICAN, 19th century
Four Wine Tasters in a Cellar. Oil painting
Gift of Maxim Karolik

Flaming Bishop

"Guaranteed to thaw frosty toes and fingers, and envelop you in a warming glow."

12-24 whole cloves
2 oranges
2 quarts port

Stick the cloves in the oranges./Roast them in a 400° oven about 20 minutes or until they begin to take on a caramel look./Cut the oranges in quarters./Add them to the port and heat *slowly* for 20-30 minutes./*Do not allow to boil.*/For added drama, remove the oranges, pour warmed Cointreau or Grand Marnier over them, set them aflame, and pour back into the port.

Miss Ellen Stillman,
Ladies' Committee Associate

Coffee Liqueur

"Make your own Kahlua at less cost. Easy to do!"

Yield: 2 quarts

3 cups sugar
4 cups water
4 heaping tablespoons instant coffee
1 fifth 100-proof vodka
1 vanilla bean, split

Simmer sugar and water 30 minutes./Mix instant coffee with one half cup of the syrup, then stir into the rest of the syrup./Cool./Add the vodka and mix well./Put ½ vanilla bean in each of 2 one-quart jars and fill with liquid./Allow to set 10 to 20 days before using.

Mrs. John A. Pooley,
Ladies' Committee

The Ultimate Eggnog

"My father's chef at the Merchants' Club in Manhattan prepared this for my family at Christmastime. There is an old saying, 'The better the brandy, the better the eggnog.' You'll see."

12 egg yolks
2 cups sugar
¼ cup powdered cloves and freshly grated
nutmeg, mixed
12 egg whites
2 quarts whipping cream
1 quart bourbon
1 pint dark rum
1 pint V.S.O.P. cognac

Beat yolks until very light./Beat in sugar, cloves, and nutmeg./Cover and let it stand overnight./Just before serving, beat egg whites stiff, beat cream until it peaks./Fold mixtures together, stir in liquor./Serve over cracked ice./Sprinkle with freshly grated nutmeg.

Maurice ("Peter") Tonissi II, Esq.,
Receptionist, Members' Room

▪ **Switchel, that old New England summer cooler, is made with a gallon of water, 2½ cups sugar, 1 cup molasses, ½ cup vinegar, and ⅔ teaspoon ginger.**

Wine and Food

Good wine and good food, together, create one of the great pleasures of life – one that is as old as history. There are fashions in foods and wines that, like all fashions, change from time to time, and our personal tastes and preferences also change and expand. Much has been written and said about choosing wines, but there is only one important criterion: if it pleases you, then it's the right choice. The flavor and aroma of wine enhance greatly the taste of food, but the joy of eating and drinking in agreeable company cannot be achieved if there is exaggerated concern over the rightness of the wine and dish. The good talk that is inseparable from a successful dinner is more important than which wines are being served. Never bring up your better bottles if you are entertaining those who cannot talk. Keep your treasures for a night when those who gather around your table will let the "wine awaken and refresh the lurking passions of the mind, as varnish does the colors which are sunk in a picture and brings them out in all their glowings" (Alexander Pope).

For your perusal and diversion and perhaps as a general guide, there follow one person's subjective thoughts on certain foods and wines that generally marry well.

Hors d'Oeuvres
Serve clean, fruity, sharp white – Sancerre Chablis, Muscadet, Alsatian, Champagne. Dry sherry goes with almost any assertive, full-flavored *hors d'oeuvre.*

Soup
If Madeira, Marsala, or sherry is used in soup, the same wine may be served.

Pasta, Rice, Grains
Usually best with red wines such as Chianti, Beaujolais, Zinfandel. Pasta with creamy white sauces would probably taste good with any wine but perhaps best with a robust red. Spicy sauces, pesto, for example, need a big sturdy red to stand up to strong flavors – a Barbera, Côte du Rhone. With fish sauce, serve a Verdicchio, Soave, or Pino Grigio.

Fish
Usually best with white wines. If dish has considerable flavor, either in flesh or sauce, match with a fairly rich-flavored wine – Meursault, white Rioja, Hermitage Blanc, Macon Blanc, California Sauvignon Blanc, or Chardonnay. For a light-flavored and subtle dish, perhaps unsauced, serve a young Moselle, Loire, or California Fumé Blanc.

Pork and Veal
A not-too-dry white wine, with some power or warmth of flavor, is best – such as an Alsatian, Rhine, or white Rhone, or a light red such as a Beaujolais or Bardolino.

Beef and Lamb
Red wines, almost always, are the optimum choice. With a stew, serve a sturdy red such as Pomerol, Saint-Emilion, Corbières, Hermitage, or California Cabernet Sauvignon. Your very best reds, such as a classified growth red Bordeaux or a Barolo, go with roasts or broiled expensive cuts of meat.

Ham
A modest young red, such as Chianti or Valpolicella, is suitable – or a slightly sweet German white such as a Rhine Spätlese.

Tripe, Brains, Liver, Tongue, Kidneys, and Sweetbreads
Try good, but not fine, red wines (Spanish, Australian or Portuguese red – Dao, Barbaresco.)

PAUL OUTERBRIDGE, JR. (American, 1896 – 1958)
Crackers and Cheese, 1922. Photograph
Gift of Thea Cottone

Chicken

Almost any wine will go with chicken, depending on how it's prepared. A young bird, plain roasted in butter, will take a really fine old red wine—Napa Cabernet Sauvignon or Chianti Classico Riserva. A chicken cooked in a wine dictates its own accompaniment. With breast meat, a white Alsatian Sylvaner or a Graves.

Game Birds

Choose your very best red wine, flowery in bouquet and rich in flavor. With domestic duck or goose, perhaps the best option would be a rather sweet white, such as an Alsatian Gewurtztraminer or a Rhine Spätlese or a soft flavored red such as a Chateauneuf-du-Pape; with wild duck, a big-scale red such as Hermitage, Burgundy, or California Cabernet Sauvignon.

Cheese

Serve your best, fine red wine, perhaps a Burgundy, only with mild cheeses. Very ripe, strong cheeses mask the flavor of really good wines and require a strong-tasting red wine such as a Rhone. Port is assertive enough to stand up to most strong cheeses. The stronger the flavor of the cheese, such as Stilton or Roquefort, the stronger or sweeter tasting the wine.

Sweet Dishes

Dessert is the most difficult food to match to a wine. (No wine goes with chocolate, sherbet, or ice cream.) Serve a truly luscious sweet Sauterne such as a Climens, Suduiraut, or Coutet of a better vintage year—as expensive as your pocketbook permits. You might enjoy sipping these Sauternes immediately after dessert if you find they please you more that way.

Notes

Acid is the enemy of wine. You can't taste wine, for instance, with the acid of grapefruit, lemon, or salad dressing containing pronounced vinegar. And yet, Salade Niçoise and other main-dish salads, with crusty bread, make delightful luncheons accompanied by any inexpensive light dry wine, either white or red.

As a general rule, if more than one wine is to be served:

- the light-bodied wine before the richer or fuller bodied
- the drier wine before the richer or sweeter wine
- the white before the red (except dessert wines)
- the younger or lesser wine usually comes first

A Word on California Wines

A suitable alternative California wine can be found for any French wine. At the level of *vin ordinaire*, California wines use the generic names borrowed from European wines to which they may have almost no resemblance—Chablis, Sauterne, Rhine, or Burgundy. The best California wines, the "premiums," however, are named after the variety of grape used, in contrast to France, where the wine is named, usually, for a geographic area and a vineyard. Some of the better California vineyards, however, have recently started labeling their *vin ordinaire* by the honest and straightforward non-French designation of "red" or "white" wine.

The Chardonnay grape in California gives wine better than most white French Burgundies in the marketplace today and the best are on the level of the greatest of the type. It can be seriously compared with fine Meursaults or even Montrachets. The Chardonnay is the top of the line in whites and makes a magnificent, complex wine in California.

Next to Chardonnay in reputation is the white Riesling, or Johannisberg Riesling—the Riesling of the Rhine and Moselle. In California, however, the Riesling grape gives a wine that is quite different from the German wines but excellent in its own characteristics – generally softer, more alcoholic, and grapier in taste.

The other white grape in California that produces a wine that can be on the same level as the white Graves of Bordeaux or the Loire wines is Sauvignon Blanc. In California, Sauvignon Blanc seems to make a fuller, richer wine. In the style of Pouilly-Fumé, the Sauvignon Blanc also makes a softer but dry version known as Dry Sauvignon or Fumé Blanc. The Chenin Blanc grape, which makes the Vouvray in the Loire, is made in a wide range of styles in California and is generally, in varying degree, sweet.

Cabernet Sauvignon, the grape of the red Bordeaux region, makes unquestionably the best American red wine. Some of them surpass most French Clarets and a few are almost as complex, subtle, and extraordinary as a first-growth Claret of a fine vintage. California generally uses the Cabernet grape 100 % – without blending – whereas red Bordeaux is made with the addition of other grape varieties to create greater complexity of flavor. A California Cabernet typically exhibits strong Cabernet character, while secondary grape varieties, when used, contribute less secondary flavors. The character of a Bordeaux, on the other hand, is a well-thought-out blend.

By and large, the Pinot Noir grape, used to make the great red wines of Burgundy, is thus far producing an undistinguished wine in California. It does not approach the quality of a fine Burgundy in the way a Cabernet Sauvignon draws near to a Bordeaux.

Zinfandel, the most widely planted varietal grape in California, has no real counterpart in any European wine. It usually makes a light, soft red of medium body, rather fruity, although some versions are heavy, intense, almost Port-like in style, or often quite similar

to a Cabernet.

Other varieties grown are the Gamay of Beaujolais (somewhat unexciting) and the Barbera of Piedmont, Italy, which produces dark, plummy, rather tart wine. The Petite Sirah is an increasingly popular variety in California. It is closely related to the Syrah of the Rhône Valley in France and produces a dark, full-bodied, and robust wine with a peppery-spicey nose. The Petite Sirah provides an intriguing change from the more common red varieties in California.

All in all, more important than what is on the label is the name of the winery that made the wine. In addition to the big, well-established familiar names, many new, small "boutique" wineries, dedicated to growing and making luxury wines of real distinction, have sprung up in California during the '70s.

Gregg B. Rains

AMERICAN, ca. 1875
Presentation goblet. Glass
Gift of Mrs. Gordon W. Hughes

Index

WILSON'S ALBANY.

Hardy, productive.

AMERICAN

ANONYMOUS AMERICAN. *Wilson's Albany* (strawberries). Stencil and watercolor from D.M. Dewey's *Nurseryman's Pocket Book of Specimen Fruit and Flowers*, 1875. Gift of Mrs. Alan Tawse

ANONYMOUS CHINESE
Branch of Loquats from the "Ten Bamboo Studio"
albums, 1633 edition
Gift of Adrian Rubel